★ OF BEARS AND BALLOTS ★

Also by Heather Lende

Find the Good

Take Good Care of the Garden and the Dogs

If You Lived Here, I'd Know Your Name

OF BEARS

★ AND ★

BALLOTS

An Alaskan Adventure in
Small-Town Politics

Heather Lende

ALGONQUIN BOOKS OF CHAPEL HILL 2020

Published by

ALGONQUIN BOOKS OF CHAPEL HILL
Post Office Box 2225
Chapel Hill, North Carolina 27515-2225

a division of

WORKMAN PUBLISHING
225 Varick Street
New York, New York 10014

This is a work of nonfiction in which some dialogue has been
reconstructed to the best of the author's recollection.

LIBRARY OF CONGRESS CATALOGING-IN-PUBLICATION DATA

Names: Lende, Heather, [date]– author.
Title: Of bears and ballots : an Alaskan adventure in
small-town politics / Heather Lende.
Description: First edition. | Chapel Hill, N.C. : Algonquin Books of
Chapel Hill, 2020. | Summary: "Following the 2016 presidential election, writer
Heather Lende, inspired to take a more active role in politics, runs for assembly
member in Haines, Alaska—and wins. But tiny Haines—a place accessible from the
nearest city, Juneau, only by boat or plane—isn't the sleepy town it appears to be.
From a bitter debate about the expansion of the fishing boat harbor to the matter
of how to stop bears from rifling through garbage to the recall campaign that
targeted three assembly members, including Lende, we witness the nitty-gritty of
passing legislation, the lofty ideals of our republic, and how the polarizing national
politics of our era play out in one small town"— Provided by publisher.
Identifiers: LCCN 2019059302 | ISBN 9781616208516 (hardcover) |
ISBN 9781643750569 (e-book)
Subjects: LCSH: Lende, Heather, [date]– | City council members—
Alaska—Haines—Biography. | City councils—Alaska—Haines. |
Haines (Alaska)—Politics and government. | Haines (Alaska)—Biography.
Classification: LCC F914.H34 L465 2020 | DDC 979.8/2—dc23
LC record available at https://lccn.loc.gov/2019059302

10 9 8 7 6 5 4 3 2 1
First Edition

For Beth

★

The mandate to exercise our civil obligations means that we can't be bystanders who scoff at the process of politics while taking no responsibility. We all need to be involved . . . It is an unpatriotic lie that we as a nation are based in individualism. The Constitution underscores the fact that we are rooted and raised in a communal society and that we each have a responsibility to build up the whole. The Preamble to the Constitution could not be any clearer: "We the People" are called to "form a more perfect Union."

—SISTER SIMONE CAMPBELL, author of *A Nun on the Bus*

Contents

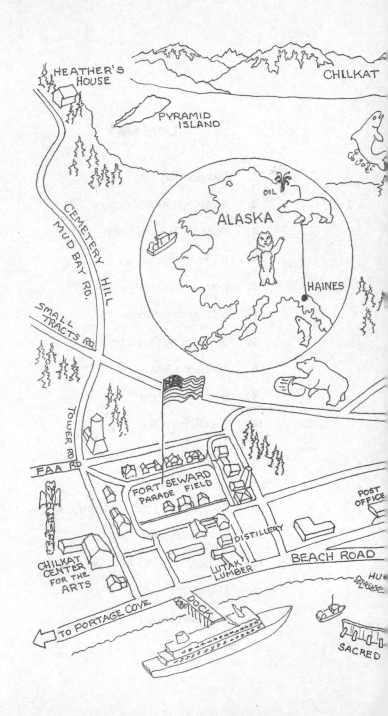

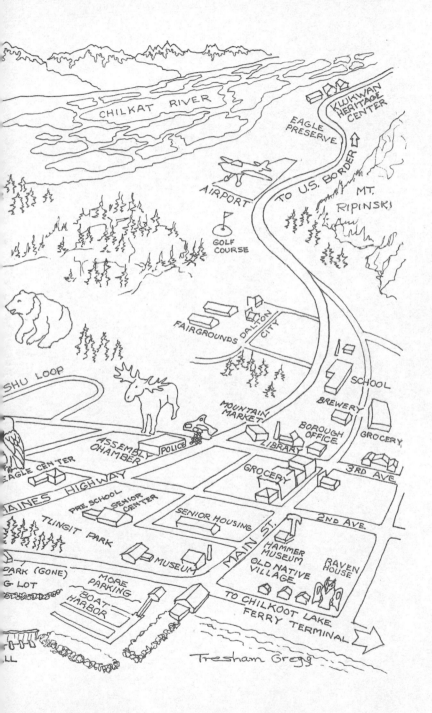

★ **OF BEARS AND BALLOTS** ★

III

From KHNS Radio
Local News in Haines, Alaska

The six candidates running for Haines Borough Assembly made the trip out to the Mosquito Lake Community Center on Wednesday night for the first forum of this local election season. About twenty Upper Valley residents gathered to ask questions and voice concerns. The candidates this year are:

Newspaper owner Tom Morphet:

"I love this town, and I love the people that live here and I wouldn't have stayed for thirty years if I didn't."

Author Heather Lende:

"I'd like to be on the assembly to say 'Why not? Yes, we can try that. Let's listen.'"

Incumbent Diana Lapham:

"Why do I want to be reelected? Three years is not long enough."

Commercial fisherman Ryan Cook:

"Everybody tries to shut down any kind of industry that starts here. I think we need some jobs."

Bookkeeper Judy Erekson:

"I've got a lot of experience with numbers, I've been doing accounting and bookkeeping for thirty, forty years."

Business owner Leonard Dubber:

"We need to cut the budget. I am definitely a budget hawk."

IIIIIIIIIIIIIIIIIIIIIIIIIIIIIIIIIIIIIIIIIIIIIIIIIIIIIIIIIIIIIIIIIIIIIIIIIIIIIIIIIIIIIIIII

★ ONE ★

Election Day

THERE ARE TWO polling places in Haines. One is in the arts center lobby, on the hill above the harbor and cruise ship dock, the other at the fire hall in Mosquito Lake, a woodsy rural settlement twenty-six miles out of town. I voted at the arts center and said hi to everyone as I walked in, but I didn't say, "Wish me luck," or anything close to it. The public radio station, KHNS, and signs on the street corners reminded residents that no campaigning was allowed at or near polling places. One neighbor, who lives in an old house with a wide porch on Soap Suds Alley, was asked by the borough clerk to remove campaign signs from his yard since his home was too close to the polls. I did notice who was there voting, though, friends and foes, and wondered which side of the Haines left-right divide would be victorious. Either way, a little more than half of us would be happy, and a little less than half would be disappointed. Haines is predictable; I assumed it would be close.

It looked to me as though more conservative voters than my supporters were at the arts center that morning. I hoped my years in town, my community service on the library board, the hospice board, and planning commission, my volunteer hosting of the local country music show on KHNS, coaching high school runners for seventeen years, five good children and five grandchildren (the sixth and seventh were still to come), our family business, Lutak Lumber, which my husband, Chip, runs, plus all those obituaries—I've been writing them for the *Chilkat Valley News* since 1997—would give me crossover support. I'm not sure that term fits Haines-style elections though. Candidates don't run on a party platform, and a so-called liberal may not want to pay more taxes for trash pickup because they recycle and compost everything, while a so-called conservative might because they are tired of illegal dumping near the river where they hunt moose. I may be a registered Democrat, but at least everyone knows me. I have written about this town in three books, which are in many ways love letters to Haines. My life is an open book, literally.

In Alaska, municipalities are organized as boroughs, and Haines Borough has a mayor, and a six-member assembly that hires a manager who runs the daily operation of what is essentially the small city that is Haines proper, with about sixteen hundred residents, and the outlying areas—the borough is about the size of Rhode Island—with a grand total of about twenty-five hundred people. I asked how the turnout had been so far, and one of the women seated at the folding table handing out ballots, a friend—our kids grew up together and we played on the same softball team—said, "Quiet but steady." That could describe any Tuesday morning in Haines. I signed the line next to my name in the big book of registered voters and took the ballot over to one of the portable red, white, and blue–curtained booths. I stopped a minute to read my own name on the official ballot before filling in the oval next to it. That little moment of pride and even joy may be as good as it gets. It could be the beginning and end of my late-in-life political career. I was proud of myself for running, for channeling my frustration with the circus of national politics that had been so distracting, really ever since Sarah Palin's rise. And now Trump seemed to be her successor in the "speak first, think later" category, prompting headlines with outrageous pronouncements and turning politics into a new kind of theater of the absurd.

After feeding my ballot into the electronic ballot box, I pressed a blue-and-yellow sticker featuring the flag of Alaska, with its Big Dipper and North Star that read I VOTED on my jacket, and we all wished one another a nice day. Which of the poll workers had voted for me, I wondered? Actually, I didn't mind not knowing. They didn't need to know who I chose, either. That's how we stay friends after an election. It is also why most businesses don't allow candidates to put up campaign signs, and why a lot of residents never endorse a candidate publicly. You don't want to burn any bridges or hurt any feelings in a place this small and isolated. Only ferries and small planes connect Haines to Juneau, the rest of southeast Alaska, and beyond, and the one road out of town runs north, through British Columbia and the Yukon Territory. I had let friends know that if they wanted to put up a yard sign, I'd give them one, or if they'd like me to come over myself and hammer it on their tree, I would. I didn't think I needed to order any more than twenty-five but ended up buying extra because of all the requests. Did they make a difference? I doubt it.

Did we even need to campaign? We candidates publicly fielded lots of questions about the biggest issues facing the community: the economy, the multi-million-dollar harbor expansion project, the freight dock repairs, the expensive private dump that results in people tossing trash out in the woods or burning it instead. I don't know if my positions changed anyone's mind. Voters knew us, and most had a first choice before any of the six candidates vying for the two open seats had even said a word. Maybe their second choice was still up for grabs.

In my thirty-plus years in Haines, a lot has changed in the national political, social, environmental, and economic climates, and those developments have in some ways coincided with shifts in our community as well. Haines has grown from an old logging and fishing town to a newer artsy place for tourists and retirees, and it's more seasonal, bustling all summer and shrinking in the winter. Hillary won Haines, as did Obama before her, though neither won in the Mosquito Lake area, which typically has about a hundred voters or less who tend to vote more right wing than left. Don Young, "Congressman for all Alaskans" forever, it seems, hasn't taken Haines a few times in recent history. It's been close, but still. Lisa Murkowski has won here every time.

The Haines electorate is violet with red and blue highlights. The Elks Club folded and is now a private gym owned by a chiropractor from Colorado with nine (or maybe ten by now) home-schooled children. There's a new distillery in a former army bakery and Leo Smith Logging Co. is no longer, and neither is Leo. The spruce that he once cut for sawmills is being used to craft custom snowboards and skis at another new business. Gift shops, tour offices, and art galleries surround his widow's trailer home and my husband Chip's lumberyard on the waterfront.

The local NRA members host an annual fundraiser at the Fogcutter Bar, where raffle prizes include assault rifles. The Southeast Alaska State Fair raffles off a new Subaru. There is a women's pistol club, where some learn to shoot in self-defense, and others for sport. My hairdresser is a member. Her husband passed away following a long illness, and she is a vocal advocate for major healthcare reform to make it affordable, compassionate, and available to all. Susan marched with the club in the Fourth of July parade wearing a sidearm in a holster buckled over her jean shorts. They meet at the public library where the environmental organization, Lynn Canal Conservation, sometimes shows films on protecting wild salmon and rivers threatened by mines, timber sales, and climate change. Bumper stickers on rigs parked on Main Street range from RESIST and BERNIE to FRIENDS DON'T LET FRIENDS EAT FARMED SALMON and EARTH FIRST, WE'LL MINE THE OTHER PLANETS LATER. On one bumper there are both INSURED BY SMITH & WESSON and IMPEACH OBAMA stickers. (They're hard to peel off after years of snow and grime.)

Here in the north, accelerated global warming is changing the landscape and altering the fisheries. No one is certain where the once-abundant Chilkat River king salmon have gone, but strict fisheries management measures are underway to keep them from disappearing altogether, including limiting commercial fishing so king salmon aren't accidentally caught with other, more plentiful species of Pacific salmon. The glaciers are retreating before our eyes, the winds blow harder, and it seems to rain more than it snows. There is a major mining prospect in the exploration phase near the headwaters of the Chilkat River, and state officials are negotiating contracts for the largest timber sales in decades. State revenue from oil development, which communities like Haines depend on for much of their funding, is waning. The Alaska Marine Highway, as the public ferry service is called, is our link to Juneau (the nearest city, more than four hours away by boat.)

It has seen reductions in service and more breakdowns than ever due to the aging fleet, all of which makes for anxious and defensive people.

A whole group of residents, including our current mayor, believe the proposed mine and increased logging activity are what Haines needs to thrive, and dream of high-paying jobs, a steady economy, and the prosperity this could bring. Writer Seth Kantner, who lives above the Arctic Circle in Kotzebue, observes that because Alaska is changing so rapidly in so many ways, we are living in the past, present, and future all at the same time. I would argue America may be as well. That's stressful. But what an opportunity this gives us to address our mutual problems together, civically, one community at a time. Climate change especially affects everyone's survival, no matter what your politics are. Or so one would think.

CAMPAIGNING MIGHT NOT have mattered but at least I enjoyed the public forums, studying local government history, and learning more about how it operates. I love the preamble to the Borough Charter and how in the Haines Borough, corporations are not people. I voted for that Charter amendment after the Citizens United ruling, along with a majority of residents on all sides of the political spectrum. It was not even controversial then, although I bet it would be now, with the mine development looming. The prospective owners are a multinational corporation seeking a louder voice in the discussion.

I've given enough book readings and talks to be comfortable in front of a crowd, but that's when I control the script and my audience is friendly, which is not always the case in campaign appearances. I was nervous in my first public forums and still am to some degree. I decided right from the get-go that I'd say exactly what I thought and not attempt to be too smooth or political by repeating tired old lines like I'd support something "if it's sustainable" or "if it's environmentally responsible" or "if it's affordable." That way there could be no big surprises if I were elected. I was happy to endorse local hiring, fully funding the library, and maintaining the pool, the school, and the nonprofits. It was easy to affirm what I like about Haines and why. The questions about government excesses and wasted tax dollars were not hard, either. Who wouldn't agree that spending twenty thousand dollars on a study confirming the helicopters used to shuttle backcountry skiers to the slopes were noisy was foolish? Or that the new—they are always new it seems—policemen need to spend less time in their cars and more time walking around, or even riding bicycles, so we get to know them and they us?

The lone incumbent who was running, Diana Lapham, argued at one forum that once you are on the assembly, decisions about studies and employees aren't so simple, because assembly members, the staff, the mayor, and the borough attorney all know more about so many things than "the general public" does. She was ignored by the rest of us who had not sat in her chair, and was even smirked at by some residents who believed that "insider information" was part of the problem with government. Later, much later, I recalled her words and understood what I believe she meant by them. Campaigning and governing are not the same at all. It's easy to say what's wrong with government; it's harder to fix it, and progress can be very slow.

• • •

THE DAY BEFORE the election, I went on a walk with my friend Margaret, who was finishing up her first year on the assembly. She brought her Lab, Buddy, and I had my golden retriever, Pearl. We met on the beach by my house, a two-mile-wide stretch of sand, meadows, and woods, with steep forested and glaciated mountains for a backdrop. A few years ago, after heated debate, the borough officially made what I think of as my backyard into the "Chilkat River Beaches Recreational Zone," including a non-motorized designation. That means no motorbikes, four-wheelers, or snow machines. I was part of that effort and was impressed by the members of the planning commission. I liked the way their meetings were run. The chair and commissioners genuinely wanted to use zoning to plan for the benefit of all and had done that with common sense and good humor. The experience prompted me to put my name in for a vacant planning commission seat.

Margaret is the reason that when my planning commission term ended, I ran for the assembly. I had encouraged her to run the year before and promised I would follow her lead the next election. We had sort of worked together at Haines's independent weekly newspaper, the *Chilkat Valley News*. She had a desk in the actual office above the bookstore and the chiropractor; I write obituaries from home. She covered the borough, schools, Chamber of Commerce meetings, car accidents, fishing, tourism, and hunting seasons, and all the other hard news. She'd gone on to be the news director at the radio station before resigning to work for a regional conservation organization.

"Who do you think will win?" I asked.

She predicted the incumbent, Diana. She thought the conservative deputy mayor, who was pro-mine and timber industry and all-in for the harbor expansion, would easily take the first seat, and the second seat would be too close to call. "Don't feel bad. You asked, and I'm just sayin'." She conceded that *maybe* I'd squeak out a victory over Ryan Cook, the young and sometimes hot-headed fisherman who agreed with Diana's positions and was less diplomatic about calling out the artists and environmentalists with whom he did not agree. He wanted to make Haines great again. But the winner might also be Judy Erekson, who did worry about the mine, and was not sure about the timber sales, and had concerns about the harbor, and was socially liberal, but was also the longtime school accountant, which gave her great value on the assembly as a budget explainer; or it might be Leonard Dubber, the libertarian plumber who could speak the same language as the borough maintenance men, and had an old-time Alaskan and anti-government vibe, somewhat eccentric views, but also a kindly, folksy way of speaking. I liked talking with him when he did the annual tune-up of our furnace.

Margaret was sure that Tom Morphet, the editor and owner of the *Chilkat Valley News*, would bring up the rear.

"Really?" I said. Tom had filed at the last possible minute, just before five o'clock on the final day because, he said, there were no competent candidates. Tom is blunt and can be rude. Times like that I wondered how we had managed to be friends for so long. He probably had no idea how much that comment stung. For better or worse, if elected, Tom and I would be viewed as a like-minded team, because we are old friends, and because of the paper and our shared relatively liberal politics. The top two vote-getters would win three-year terms. The seats are staggered so that the entire assembly and mayor won't shift too drastically year-to-year, and to provide continuity with at least two senior members, two two-year members, and two freshman members on any assembly—or at least that's the theory.

"I don't think we will have the results tonight; absentee ballots will decide it," Margaret said.

"Are you sure?"

"My guess is it will probably be Diana and then you when it's all sorted out. It may take a while is all."

Maybe I should have campaigned harder. I had spent about a thousand dollars and thought that was too much. Half of it was for the signs, and the rest for ads in the paper. I never held a fundraiser. How could I solicit money from someone now and then disagree with them later? It doesn't take a political scientist to explain how money influences Congress. How can it not? Mainly I talked to people informally and answered questions at a handful of the candidate forums sponsored by the Chamber of Commerce, newspaper and radio station, and the miners.

My Mud Bay Road neighbor who had advised many Alaska politicians suggested that I "never speak in absolutes." He said that if I declared I will or won't do this or that, I'd set myself up, and to some extent the assembly I join, for failure. Especially when campaigning, it was critical to keep an open mind and listen to concerns and ideas that I might address later as an assembly member.

When I was on the planning commission, I had opposed the multi-million-dollar harbor expansion project because I had doubts about the design, but I was the lone dissenter so the engineer's plan was approved by the commission and then by the previous assembly. Now that same plan was going out for bids and the new assembly would have to make the final decision. (Committees and commissions are advisory to the assembly, which has the last word since they alone have the authority to appropriate the funds.) While campaigning I backed off some. I was still against it, but partly I was trying to heed the advice of my neighbor, and partly I had decided a borough-wide advisory vote—a referendum—would be fairest. Then we'd know for sure what people wanted. If the planning commission and the old assembly and the Ports and Harbor Committee were right, and I and the other detractors were wrong, the voters would approve it and we'd move on, confident that a majority had ruled.

On this point Margaret disagreed with me. She was for moving ahead with construction without delay. She'd worked on the harbor design for the last year and thought my fears, and others', about the final price tag, the maintenance costs of the steel breakwater, and the necessity of the huge parking lot, were unfounded.

AT THE ALASKA Miners Association's candidate forum at seven o'clock on a Friday morning in the Pioneer Bar, I answered the first question about any personal connection to mines or mining we may have by divulging that my great-grandfather had been a Klondike prospector, and that my grandfather was a mining engineer who graduated from the Colorado School of Mines and worked in the coal, oil, and gas country of Western Pennsylvania. There's a photo by my desk of a great-grandmother on my mother's side seated sidesaddle on a burro at the Mexican silver mine where she taught school. Borough and burro. Was it a sign?

I told the audience that I loved songs about mining like "Sixteen Tons" (but didn't mention John Prine's "Paradise," about a Kentucky town that Mr. Peabody's coal train hauled away) and literature inspired by mining, from stories like "The Luck of Roaring Camp" to the writings of Jack London and Robert Service, whose classics, or at least lines from them, Alaskans are familiar with. One of my favorite novels is Wallace Stegner's *Angle of Repose*. The book is about love and a marriage and is set in Western mining towns. The title is a metaphor, but in reading the book, I learned that practically speaking, "angle of repose" is the term for the steepest slope at which a hill of loose material, say mine tailings or gravel, is stable. When the phrase was mentioned in a planning commission review of a gravel pit, I knew what it was, thanks to that novel. I was so eager to please, that I may have even told the miners that they could borrow my copy of the book, if they wanted to read it. Some of them work in mining camps near Juneau; others are part of the Constantine Metal Resources crew exploring that potential mine in Haines.

"You probably shouldn't mention literature next time," my campaign manager, Teresa, said as we debriefed over a glass of prosecco in my kitchen.

"That's the least of our worries," I said, and told her what happened when the moderator asked if I supported a so-called Tier 3 clean water designation, the highest protection possible for the Chilkat River, which is right below the Constantine mine site. When the moderator said, "Yes or no, one word," Diana said no, Leonard said no, Ryan said no, Judy said she wasn't sure but when pressed said no reluctantly.

"Heather?"

"Yes."

"You said yes?" Teresa asked. "To the miners?"

"Yes."

"Well. Good for you," she said.

Never mind that another old and dear friend, road-building contractor Roger Schnabel, my daughter JJ's godfather, put his head in hands and said, "Oh, no, Heather, and I was going to vote for you."

Tom said, "Yes," and loudly, too.

Was this why Margaret thought we might be doomed?

|||||||||||||||||||||||||||||||||||||||||||||||||||||||||||||||||||||||||||||||||||||||

Candidates Answer Questions
from the *Chilkat Valley News*

Should the police force be reduced?

Erekson, Cook, Morphet, and Dubber want to trim the number. "If there is a drug problem, we can deal with that with treatment. . . . Let's try something new," Morphet said.

Lende and Lapham voiced concerns about drugs in Haines. "There is an underbelly to Haines that we normally don't hear about," Lende said.

Should Haines hold a referendum on proceeding with the harbor improvements?

Erekson, Lende, Morphet, and Dubber support a referendum.

Cook and Lapham oppose a referendum, arguing the borough should proceed immediately with the first phase, which includes installing a steel breakwater, filling in the uplands, and possibly converting much of that area into a parking lot. They argued that the design has already gone through years of public input and modifications.

|||||||||||||||||||||||||||||||||||||||||||||||||||||||||||||||||||||||||||||||||||||||

★ TWO ★

Running for Office

MY SON, CHRISTIAN, thought I was nuts. My four daughters didn't encourage me, either. When I said I wanted my grandchildren to remember how I jumped into local government, and that maybe I would be an example for one of them to do the same, that one of the little girls playing in my living room while I talked campaign strategy on the phone would grow up to be president, Sarah and Stoli, who both live in Haines with their families, raised their eyebrows. It's the same look they give me when I suggest they take up cycling and ride with Chip and me. Have I mentioned that my husband Chip crashed just a few years after I was run over by a truck? So we've both broken our pelvis. I nearly died; Chip's accident wasn't as bad, but just as scary initially and, like mine, involved an emergency medevac flight to Seattle. There is no hospital in Haines.

Whenever I remind Christian to be safe, he laughs and says that we've been more seriously hurt riding bikes than he ever has in one of the most dangerous professions in the world, commercial fishing, and surfing among great white sharks. He's in Australia doing just that right now. When I asked my oldest daughter Eliza, an elementary school teacher in Juneau who's currently taking a break to be with her young children for a few years and do the books for her husband's physical therapy practice, if I should run, she said, "No." So did JJ, who added, "But if you really want to, go for it." That's my girl. She became an elementary school principal at twenty-six. JJ is full-in with all she does.

Chip had been on the old Haines City Council for fifteen years and also served one term on the borough assembly after the two governments united and formed the current assembly. I bet he could have been elected forever. He chose to leave because he realized life was too short to spend it sitting in front of disagreeable people. No one comes to meetings because they are happy with the government, he told me. Instead, he became the treasurer for the all-volunteer Haines Arts Council. They bring in performers from around the country, even the world, such as the BodyVox dance troupe, the Moscow Chamber Orchestra, and the Hot Club of Cowtown country jazz band. "The best part of being on the arts council is that if people don't like what we're doing, then they don't have to buy a ticket, and they never come just to complain from the front row," he says.

I didn't really hear Chip's concerns, and I brushed off my kids' warnings about not running. I turned in my paperwork, a declaration of intent to run for office with ten signatures on it, including Chip's, to the borough clerk as soon as the filing period opened at the end of July. "I won't say 'I told you so,' if you are elected and it's no fun at all," Chip said. (Hardly a ringing endorsement.) Then I headed straight out of town to Tenakee Springs.

The only access to the tiny, mostly-vacation-homes village is by ferry or floatplane. There are no roads, so residents walk, ride old bikes, or use four wheelers on the waterfront path lined with small houses and a boardwalk. Teresa used to teach in the Tenakee school (it's now closed) before she and her husband, Larry, moved to Haines about the same time we did. They kept their house and the island connections. Months before I decided to run and she agreed to be my campaign manager, Teresa asked if I would be her guest for the annual summer Tenakee Book Club meeting. She explained that they always bring in a guest author for a week and wine and dine them, and since I'm her friend, the club members thought perhaps she could convince me, and we'd take hikes and soak in the hot spring.

"Are you kidding me? I'd love to come. I had no idea you were proud of me."

"Oh, stop," Teresa said, laughing. "And don't let it go to your head."

The internet in Tenakee is painfully slow and the cell phone reception just as spotty, but Teresa and I managed to design and order campaign signs for me from a Juneau printer using a landline. We didn't have much time. They'd take a few weeks to arrive, it would be August when I returned home, and the election was October 4. The printer asked who my campaign manager was, so I looked across the cabin and asked her what I should say, and she replied it should be her, naturally. "You will need all the help you can get."

I just now realized that Teresa may be my oldest friend, or my longest friend, since I don't know how old she is and she is not telling. Our oldest daughters are the same age and will be thirty-five this year. Her son went to school with my second daughter, Sarah. JJ worked with Teresa when she was a long-term substitute teacher at her school. Teresa speaks with her hands and invokes saints and

Mary and Joseph and the pope when she speaks. When she loses something she prays to St. Anthony, the patron saint of lost objects, and some might say lost souls. I love the informal version of the plea used by a Jewish friend of ours: "Tony, Tony, look around, something's lost and can't be found," and Teresa laughs when I use that one. Actually, she laughs all the time and is the best dinner guest in the world because she makes everyone feel welcome. She is bossy, too, in a teacher-knows-better sort of way. Everybody likes being with her. I couldn't imagine a better campaign manager.

Before we took a bath, she handed me a towel, a bar of soap in a baggie, and a washcloth, which I stuffed in a canvas sack with my toiletries and clean underwear, and the flip-flops she had also told me to pack, and we climbed onto ratty old bikes. It was my first visit to Tenakee, but I had heard about the communal bathhouse at the hot spring. Southeast Alaska is challenging to travel because there are no roads between communities, and ferry schedules to the tiny village require overnighting in Juneau and staying a minimum of a week. Teresa and Larry visit Tenakee on holidays with their family at the same time I'm with mine, and the cabin is small, so a visit never worked out until then. I don't know where the time went, but my hair has turned gray and Teresa is retired and neither one of us remember much about our thirties.

Teresa's bicycle looked to be in a little better shape than mine. She is addicted to garage sales and brings home broken appliances, furniture, and apparently these guest bicycles. Larry is a retired contractor and he does the repairs. "The chain falls off if you keep your feet on the pedals when you are coasting, so just stick your legs out when you slow down," he instructed. The bathhouse is a small concrete building next to the store and the ferry dock. We leaned the bikes against the fence and stepped into an old-fashioned wooden locker room with wainscoting and gray painted benches and hooks for our clothing. A sign on the door into the bath, as the spring is called, proclaims No SWIMSUITS ALLOWED. NUDE BATHING ONLY.

When I asked Teresa why no swimsuits, she said there are separate hours for men and women, which didn't really answer the question. I started to open the door to the bath wrapped in a towel, but Teresa, who wore nothing but flip-flops, said to toss it on the bench as she marched by me. I hesitated, then followed. I had pictured the antique bathhouse sheltering a steamy creek with deep natural pools. I'd guessed there would be a dim, candlelit grotto with ferns and the tinkling sounds of water. Instead I looked down from the top of a steep stairway at the 6- by 9-foot concrete-trimmed tank over a hole in the rocky bottom where the spring welled up. It felt like an old, very damp basement except it was hot, and bright, thanks to the large steamy skylight. The pool tilted slightly and cleaned itself by overflowing across the mossy floor and out a hole in the wall to the beach. It smelled of hard-boiled eggs. The gray-green light sort of reminded me of old Italian paintings, and I hoped it would be as flattering. Oh dear. Breathe.

When in Tenakee, do as the Romans.

There were a couple of other naked women cooling off on the edge of the tub and stretching out in it. One I recognized. Linda and I are kind of related, since I married her son. I mean, I actually performed the ceremony when Jimmy wed my neighbor's daughter. They have two little boys now and live on a military base. Jimmy is career army and had just returned from a tour in Afghanistan.

Linda usually wears a lot of layers. Skirts, leggings, scarves, hats, and jingling jewelry. She teaches music. She has also prayed with the Dalai Lama, sings, writes poetry and marches for peace. I did not even mention our nudity when I started to ease into the pool next to her. The water was gin clear.

"Heather!" Teresa nearly shouted. "Use your soap and wash-cloth first!" I'd thought she'd given them to me for the bath. Turns out you clean off *before* you bathe. Teresa filled a couple of milk jugs and a plastic Folgers coffee container with water from the pool and motioned me to do the same, and we moved toward the downhill side of the room. She instructed me to wash my ears, the back of my neck, arms, and legs, everywhere, then dump hot water on myself to rinse off the soap. "We need to keep the bath clean for everyone else."

I was scrubbing off more than dead skin. I was contributing to a common good. Tenakee has a city council, and the bath is a community asset, but the care of it depends on the good faith of the users. I like that. I'm trying to be, I want to be, the kind of woman who says, and believes, that she can change the world through small acts, in small places, and have enough confidence—or is the word "wisdom"?—to actually do it. Now I tell myself that I should be grateful to have a body that has born children, run over mountains, and survived accidents and surgeries and still works well, most of the time. A body I am happy to live in and be proud of just the way it is. (Don't spit your tea out, and I forgive you for saying "You've *got* to be kidding.")

I'm actually serious. If not now, when? If I'm going to put myself out there politically, for everyone to examine and critique, I better make sure I'm comfortable in my own skin. I slid in the pool and gasped. "It's 106 degrees," Linda said. She was floating on her back. She invited us to her yoga class the next day. Teresa slipped in as I sat up on the ledge to cool off. I felt great.

A younger woman came and went, as did a much older woman. Everyone washed and soaked and talked, our nakedness incidental, unimportant. They all said they'd be attending the book club meeting and they did, I think. I may not have recognized some with dry hair and shirts. The Tenakee reading was different from any other I have done, and not just because I was light-headed from the hot baths. I was more careful about how I delivered my stories about writing obituaries and what remains when we lose everything and finding the good in life's struggles because I had seen my audience bare all, and they had seen me. I was more aware of the scars that are usually hidden. Of how tender those places are that we usually don't expose. What if every community had a public bath? How much kinder would we be to one another?

A few soaks later a woman who hadn't been at the book club arrived. She had thick, white, shoulder-length hair and looked familiar. The chat was the same as always, friendly and welcoming, on topics like the weather, or the bakery hours, or a bear on the trail out by the bridge. On the way home, wobbling with my legs sticking out straight on the bike as we coasted past the one-room post office, Teresa said that the woman was a state lawmaker, the same one who had recently been in the news for writing letters of support in the trial of two men who were convicted of multiple accounts of sexually assaulting a child. Apparently she knew them from her church, and they had asked for her help. Now, she was about to lose her seat in the legislature in the fall election and had probably come back to the family place in Tenakee to avoid the news. The lawmaker had probably wanted to do a good deed. She followed her heart and not her head. She must not have done her homework. "Remember this," I told myself. It's fine to believe the best of people, but if I become a politician, people may use my goodwill for their benefit, so I shouldn't assume my supporters are always right or even share my values. My mother was an avid reader but used to remind us that this did not make her a good person, pointing out that Hitler read a lot, too.

ON ELECTION DAY, after Chip came home from work and we were having a drink together before dinner, I asked him who he thought would win. "You and Tom," he said.

I shared Margaret's thoughts.

"I see a lot of people in the store from all walks. They're voting for Tom because he speaks his mind and doesn't worry about what anyone thinks about him. They're voting for you because you care a lot about this town and will give it your all."

"You are just saying that because you love me."

"It's also why it won't be the end of the world if Margaret is right."

THE ELECTION RESULTS were certainly taking long enough to come in over the radio. The polls closed at eight and it was almost ten. I'd already been over to my neighbor Linnus's, where a few other friends had gathered to wait. It wasn't a party exactly, but almost. A handful of us sat around her kitchen table drinking wine and listening to KHNS, making guesses on the outcome. Tom came by, too. But it was late and I was tired, so I walked home by the light of a headlamp and slipped quietly into my side of the bed, pushing Pearl to the floor, turning the radio on low so as to not wake Chip.

The campaign had exposed deep divisions over the harbor project and the proposed Constantine mine, and also, just as the national presidential campaign had, something else that was harder to define but in a way was related to those two. I hesitate to name it, because there are always exceptions, and I'm afraid that if I do, then I will be part of the problem. Yet there was something more happening here than the issues in this campaign, and that something had to do with Us and Them and Old and New, even, as it had in the national presidential campaign, the People and the Government.

One candidate drew nods of approval every time he said we needed to cut the budget fat, that there were too many people working for the borough, and they were paid too much. Those same employees are our friends and neighbors. It's not as if they wouldn't be hurt by such talk. If I did win, I wondered how I could be both responsible as a leader and also mindful of their needs. One candidate, Ryan, spoke about returning Haines to the good old sawmill days and recalled his grandpa driving a log truck and how everyone was happy, and the town wasn't divided like it is now. He was in school with my children, so he could have only heard those stories second-hand, not lived them. The same must be true of Trump voters who forget that coal mines are not the best places to work. That much I knew from my grandfather's side of the family.

After the polls closed, a half-dozen local women who had served as the election officials counted the ballots for the clerk (with the help of the voting machines). The clerk releases the unofficial results to the radio station as soon as they are finished. Every election, it always takes longer than I think it will. Margaret must have been surprised when the radio announcer read the preliminary results. I had won and Tom had beaten Diana by ten votes. Ryan, Judy, and Leonard followed.

A week later, a meeting was held to canvass, or count, the last straggling absentee ballots and affirm that the election was conducted properly, with the assembly serving as the canvass board. The mayor called the meeting to order, explained the procedure, and then opened the absentee ballot envelopes and read the names each voter selected for both of the contested assembly seats. There were a lot of "Lende, Morphets," and the two available school board seats were primarily "Schwartz, Swinton." That's Lisa, a nurse at the clinic, and Sarah who manages her family's grocery store. The assembly members, working in pairs—one reading, one writing—counted the votes for each candidate, marking a line for every four, and after the slash for the fifth giving a collective cry of "tally." The clerk double-checked the figures and caught any mistakes.

The candidates, as well as everyone else who was interested, sat in the audience and watched. Seven hundred and ninety-seven ballots were cast in person on October 4, and another 204 absentee ballots that had been received by then were also counted by election workers and the clerk that night. The last thirty were counted now, the assumption being that all mailed ballots should be back in Haines a week after the deadline. The final election results would be sent on to the assembly to certify at the regular meeting on October 25, which would also be when the two winners were sworn in.

This is all according to local law, which is the Haines Borough Code. The clerk, following the Code and state and federal guidelines, supervises elections. So while it may seem silly and like a lot of work for everyone in such a small place, with only eight hundred households whose occupants cast a total of 1,032 votes, where there are no issues of fraud or foreign interference, and especially when the count won't alter the outcome, having rules, and laws, and following them, from the bottom up, no matter who the personalities are, is serious business.

So much depends on the integrity and honesty of the people who oversee the electoral process. This is why I stick a flag in the tub of pansies at the end of my driveway every Fourth of July. But there's more. Once an election is certified, citizens agree to abide by the decision of the majority. When all was said and done, I won with 501 votes, and Tom had 436. Alekka Fullerton, the new deputy borough clerk, a retired attorney from California who had visited Haines on vacation and fallen in love with it, stood up during the public comment section of the agenda. When she said how grateful she was to live in a community where election officials make sure every single vote counted, her voice cracked. This is democracy, she said. This is America. This matters. Haines doesn't realize what we have here, and how fortunate we are to have such an engaged citizenry.

She's right, I thought. The election process, taken seriously, in the smallest of communities, is what our country is all about. Then I teared up. I was so proud and happy to win, it was all I could do not to stand up like Sally Field at the Oscars and say, "You like me!" and it was even better to be included in a small chapter of a much larger history-making story. I was excited that I would be in office when voters around the country chose our first woman president in a month. My granddaughters would indeed tell this tale someday. To celebrate I will give them photographs of me sitting in my borough chair and copies of the one of their great-great-grandmother on that burro, taken back before women could vote, to hang next to each other in their hallways someday.

Well, we all know how that turned out. But I want to preserve that moment of optimism and hope. I want to be sure you know, and that I won't forget, how much winning the election meant to me. Grandma Mimi was about to become Haines Borough Assembly Member Lende. How about that?

From KHNS Radio Local News:

Alaska's official results are in for the [national] Nov. 8 election. They don't significantly change the picture of which candidates Northern Lynn Canal voters preferred. Most [voters in Haines, Skagway, and Klukwan] favored Democrat Hillary Clinton for president but Republican incumbents for Alaska offices.

Haines Precinct 2 [the Mosquito Lake area] is the only Upper Lynn Canal district that favored Trump. Half of the 96 voters cast ballots for the GOP nominee. About 38 percent went for Clinton. Fourteen percent voted for a third-party or write-in.

All Upper Lynn Canal districts favored Republican Lisa Murkowski for US Senate.

THREE

Robert's Rules of Order

As a new assembly member I was not given any orientation at all, except for a brief lesson from the clerk and the tech guy on how to use my borough-issued iPad, which they told me contained everything I needed to know, from my official email address (yes, even in Haines we're not supposed to use private email accounts for public business) to the Borough Code, meeting minutes and agendas, the calendar, and more.

There were no explicit instructions to use surnames with appropriate titles instead of first names when addressing others in the chambers, but I had sat through enough meetings as a civilian to understand the way residents and officials (like me, now) spoke to one another. Assembly meetings are the most structured of all local meetings. The monthly library board business meetings, which I had attended for years, were a coffee klatch by comparison. Library board members made simple motions and seconds, and voted with a "yes" to approve the treasurer's report, or closing for a day to clean the carpets, or hiring a part-time circulation desk clerk for the busy summer months when cruise ship passengers use the library's Wi-Fi and the children's reading program is in full swing. We called the library director "Patty" and one another by our first names.

The only place in Haines where Mr., Ms., Miss, or Mrs. are normally used is at the school. My children always called their art teacher Ms. Danner in her classroom, but she's our friend and neighbor and is Linnus outside of school. Even teachers we're not so close to are on a first-name basis with my kids (and likely most students) on Main Street or at Mountain Market. There have been a few exceptions to the first name custom. I used to call the Catholic priest Father Blaney even though he said, "Call me anything except late for dinner." He always wore his white collar, even riding his bicycle twenty miles to Chilkoot Lake and back, and demonstrated a friendly, Irish village clergyman kind of authority that made Father Blaney ring truest. He died a few years ago of cancer. It was, as he would say, blessedly quick.

I am probably not the only former patient who still reflexively calls our longtime Haines family physician Dr. Jones, even though he no longer practices medicine and now owns a nine-hole golf course. He had never played a round of golf when, well into his seventies, he decided to build a course on riverfront property near town. (He's now almost ninety.) I saw Dr. Jones for prenatal appointments during my childbearing years and the title may have been his way—I know it was this patient's way—of keeping what happens in the clinic at the clinic. The formality allowed me to sort of forget that he had given me a pelvic exam a few hours before a church potluck we both went to, and he certainly never mentioned it. It helped remind both of us that health matters were private, and that made living, and in his case working, in such a small town more comfortable. Old habits are hard to break, so even though more people now know him as Stan, when I'm golfing (I learned on his course) and he drives by on the mower I shout, "Hi, Dr. Jones." He can't hear me but he waves back anyway.

A little courtesy goes a long way toward maintaining dignity and a sense of security. Formal manners can also remind all of us to be mindful of the words and actions we choose. One way the process of governing is made more efficient and ensures everyone is afforded the kind of respect with which Dr. Jones treated me is to adhere to *Robert's Rules of Order. The Rules* were first published in 1876 by US Army General Henry Martyn Robert and have had at least eleven printings since then with over five million copies in circulation today. A few meetings into my term, it became apparent that some of us did not know the rules as well as others, and that even the people who thought they had them down cold were making mistakes. Assembly members were given *The Complete Idiot's Guide to Robert's Rules, Second Edition* by Nancy Sylvester, who sings the praises of proper parliamentary procedure. (I know; it's the Idiot's Guide. I tried not to take offense.) The author contends that sticking to the rules will shorten meetings, protect minority voices, and that when faced with controversies, the formality of the language and protocol should keep the assembly focused on issues rather than the personalities of the people debating for and against proposed solutions.

I think she is right. Although using *Robert's Rules* can sometimes make me feel as if I'm in a Monty Python sketch: "I move to amend the amendment to the amendment of the main motion to read 'up to' not 'to' in line three, letter F on page four of ordinance number 17-02-488." Or . . . whatever. For handy reference, in our folders at every meeting there's a list of motions and the order in which they should be made, beginning with the simplest and progressing to the most complex. A basic motion that allows a discussion and then a vote on an agenda item may be: "I move to adopt ordinance number 18-01-487 to amend Title 8 Section 8.08.020 and Title 15 to require burning permits in all service areas. Is there a second?" The mayor looks around and nods to the person with their hand up and after that person says, "Second," the mayor opens the public hearing and takes comments from residents who have signed up at the beginning of the meeting to talk to us.

Speakers are allowed a maximum of three minutes, timed by the clerk. When everyone has had a say, the mayor gavels the public hearing closed, and the debate over the question of approval or not comes back to the assembly. The mayor calls on assembly members who speak for or against it. Around the time when we are all repeating ourselves, she calls for "the Question." That's shorthand for "it's time to make a decision, answer the question we have been debating 'yea' or 'nay,' and move on." Sometimes it is a simple show of hands; other times, especially for major decisions, there is a roll call vote, in which the clerk asks each of us by name how we vote. "Assembly Member Lende?" "Yes." And so forth. If passed, the motion becomes Haines Borough's official position or law, no matter how we voted as six individuals. In the event of a tie, the mayor casts the deciding vote.

In addition to addressing all members of the audience or staff present as Mr. and Ms., their title, if they have one—such as Manager or Harbormaster—should be used. If they are an appointed committee member or commissioner, I say, "Commissioner Goldberg" or "Committee Chair Chapell," instead of "Rob" or "Rich." Or at least I try and remember to. At some meetings there are twenty or thirty people—these are usually the controversial ones. If the agenda is fairly tame, there could be five people total, including the reporters for the radio and paper.

I initially chafed at some of this stuff; it seemed a little silly. Tom Morphet and I are friends. He calls me Heath and I call him Tommy sometimes. Most friends and enemies know him as Morphet. He has more of the former, as his election proved, but the latter are passionate thanks to years of opinionated editorials at the paper he owned. He especially challenges people in power, such as public officials, business leaders, bar owners, school superintendents, borough managers, police officers, and large-scale tour operators. He demands to know how public money is spent and why. He sticks up for the marginalized. And he doesn't like to follow rules.

Tom volunteered for years as a Big Brother to a troubled young man whom he still takes care of; rings the bell for the Salvation Army kettle in the grocery store at Christmas; plays taps on his trumpet at funerals and in the funky marching band he organized for parades, just because he thought Haines should have one. Tom's wife is an independent, sunny Australian who is as calm and soft-spoken as Tom is bold and loud. Tom and I often disagree and drive each other crazy but he could be my brother—that's how I feel about him. I worked for Tom for decades at the *Chilkat Valley News*, which he said he would sell when he ran for office. That took a while and caused some problems, which you will learn later is an understatement. But for now, I'll just leave it that addressing Tom as Assemblyman Morphet, or even Mr. Morphet, has been very weird.

Once, when Chip and I walked into a Juneau hotel lounge for dinner, we were thrilled to see Madam Clerk, aka Julie Cozzi, from

Haines with her auburn hair very styled, swaying in a sparkly white gown, and crooning "Fly Me to the Moon." We stayed for the whole set. She's terrific on stage. On the dais at assembly meetings, Clerk Cozzi is more subdued. She doesn't sing there. Ever. Or wear makeup. She is serious and thoughtful, and she and the mayor, Jan Hill, sit next to each other and whisper back and forth instructions that no one else can hear. At choir practice or when watching high school basketball games the mayor is Jan, but at meetings she is Madam Mayor or sometimes, if we forget, Mayor Hill.

Jan is Tlingit and her Alaska Native ancestors settled in this region long before there were national boundaries or English was even spoken in Alaska for that matter, and since Haines is only forty miles from Canada, she enjoys cultural gatherings with her many tribal relatives and friends in the Yukon Territory. After returning from an event in Whitehorse, she noted with a smile that in Canada mayors are addressed as "Your Worship" and that she liked it. I joked that we could call her "Your Highness" and she smiled again. *Robert's Rules* dictate that the mayor, who is "the chair," decides who may speak and in what order. I must be "recognized by the chair" or remain silent. The mayor is conservative and supports the mining and timber industries, and does not identify with the many local Tlingits who oppose such development as a threat to their traditional way of life, which is dependent on the bounty of nature. She had also hoped her deputy mayor, Diana, would be elected for another term and supported her candidacy. A couple of times while I was waiting my turn to speak—and I was often waiting my turn in the first year on the job, because Jan seemed to keep me, and especially Tom, at the bottom of her list, perhaps because we were usually 180 degrees apart from her politically—I almost said, "Please Mother may I?" instead of "Madam Mayor, may I speak?"

I did enjoy addressing my friend and fellow assembly member Margaret as Ms. Friedenauer, because it elevated her to a position of authority that I felt she had earned. She is younger than I am, still in her thirties, but wiser in the ways of politics, and whip-smart. In addition to her local reporting work, Margaret has written for large papers in Alaska and New Mexico and was embedded with the troops in Iraq on one assignment. Originally from Montana, she married a Haines fisherman and photographer, and lives near me on Mud Bay Road.

When my term began, Mayor Hill made former mayor Mike Case the deputy mayor, which meant he chaired meetings in her absence. He'd become an assembly member two years before me. Assemblyman Case is a Vermonter, and I went to college there, so we have that connection. He's over eighty years old, and a widower. He was so kind as a caregiver for his chronically ill wife it was inspiring. After Mike saw me struggling and frustrated in the first few meetings, he offered to give me a tutorial on all things borough, from *Robert's Rules* to how to amend ordinances. I appreciated that he was the last mayor to insist that we paint the fire hall, and that he chose the colors to match our award-winning library, a rusty-cedar tone with blue-gray trim. He also had the same paint applied to the administration building, to identify them all as borough facilities.

The library and admin building have held up well. They're relatively new or recently remodeled, but the fire hall, which is old and decrepit and also houses the police department and assembly chambers, looks awful. It's a big sagging box with a flat roof surrounded by a large, mostly dirt parking lot. Some hanging flower baskets appear in the summer by the police station door and the assembly chambers entrance, but they almost make it worse by calling attention to the place. A weathered Tlingit-carved killer-whale sculpture sits on the corner, and on a nearby flagpole fly the Stars and Stripes and Alaska's state flag.

Four mayors and more managers than that later, no one has had the will to repaint the old plywood shell as Mike had done. It costs plenty, more than $150,000. The opponents of repainting always use that awful "lipstick on a pig" line; well, sometimes a cosmetic makeover can do wonders for self-esteem, and you can't put a value on that. I feel a lot better when my toenails are polished, even if they are tucked into my socks and rubber boots, and no one ever sees them but me. At least everyone agrees that the building needs to be replaced, but Haines does not have ten or twelve million dollars to pay for it. Construction grants have been applied for but not awarded, and emergency repairs have been made, but Mike's paint is peeling now and the building is an eyesore in the center of town. It's more than ironic since the volunteer fire and ambulance department is something residents love and are proud of. Lipstick indeed.

Maybe it's best that Assemblyman Case can't see how shabby it has become, as his eyesight is failing. I'd love to see that building fixed up, but I don't have the votes on the assembly to convince the others to pay for it, yet. Maybe that's a battle I will never win.

This might be a good place to acknowledge that I'm conflicted about using the gender-specific term "assemblyman" or "assemblywoman." I still prefer these terms to "assembly member," even if they are sexist. I've heard more than a few guys utter "Assembly

Member Morphet" in a less than respectful tone. I raised five teen-agers, so my brain chemistry has been altered, and this kind of a moment can cause me to snort my water. When I do, I half expect Margaret . . . I mean my good friend Assemblywoman Friedenauer to stage whisper my way, "Pick your mind up out of the gutter, Lende. Whoops, I mean Assembly *Member* Lende." Then again, senators in Washington actually do say, "My good friend the senior senator from the great state of Nevada," because it's tra-dition, even though they don't always mean "good," "friend," or "great." I've read that Mitch McConnell and Harry Reid used to practically spit "my good friend" at each other.

Another actual good friend on the dais is Tresham Gregg, an artist, performer, and puppeteer with a self-described "groovy vibe" that does not match "Mr. Gregg" or Assemblyman or Assembly Member Gregg at all. Tresham is like Cher. One name is all he needs. His father was also a Tresham but was always called Ted. Ted was an army officer from Connecticut and part of the veterans group that purchased Fort Seward in Haines after WWII and moved their families into the big white houses with wide front porches up on Officers Row overlooking the parade grounds and harbor. Tresham lives in one of those grand old homes now, although he was never a military man. He's a pacifist and chose Canada over Vietnam. He owns several art galleries, and also paints, carves, and makes jewelry. He designs his own colorful clothes.

The year before Tom and I were elected, Tresham decided out of the blue to run for assembly and defeated a long-time conser-vative former mayor (not Mike, but a guy named Jerry; I told you we are a very active political town). Even his friends and family

(Tresham's son is a Stanford-educated attorney with the Justice Department) thought he would be trounced—especially with his economic development plan to market Haines as *the* place to be for art therapy, puppet shows, and vision quests. His win indicated that our town had slid left of center before Tom and I were even elected.

I did not know much about Ron Jackson when I joined the assembly, only that he was a quiet man with a nice smile, and that what I saw on the Lilly Lake trail whenever I bumped into him snowshoeing, I liked. A more recent transplant to Haines, Ron retired here with his wife and a cocker spaniel from the Pacific Northwest, where he had worked for the Forest Service. Ron's pleasant, thoughtful demeanor, down vests, and jeans did not shout authority figure, or Assemblyman Jackson, but that's what I call him, because those are the rules, and I follow them, even though this is Haines, and Alaska, where the local physician is no longer Dr. Jones (she goes by Lylith), and where everyone knows that the Honorable Senator Lisa Murkowski is simply Lisa.

Still, when two months into our term, during the public comments at the end of a meeting, the rules flew out the window, for a moment anyway, I was shocked. Former assembly member Ms. Diana Lapham called Assemblyman Morphet "Tom" and added that he was despicable and furthermore should take off his hat and respect the flag when he said the Pledge of Allegiance. Someone else in the audience made a crack under his breath about Tresham's lack of patriotism. The simmering anger from some residents about the surprise election results and the controversial early choices the new assembly had made seemed to be playing out and everything became personal, quickly.

Shouting "Tom" instead of "Assemblyman Morphet" may not sound like a big deal. Some people might believe that breaching snooty protocols is refreshing and honest. Some people might applaud, and some did. Was this related to the way President Trump smacked down both colleagues and challengers, ignoring niceties or even the implied dignity of the office of the president as he campaigned? The influence of right-wing talk radio chat? (There is now, finally, satellite service in Haines, so not everyone listens to the only station, public radio KHNS, which airs NPR news, anymore. I bet many don't.) Is it the effect of the internet and Facebook making space for anonymous and not-so-anonymous bullies and thugs that comment crudely on everything? I don't know. I do know that as 2016 rolled into 2017, 2018, and 2019, the assembly chambers, and politics in Haines, like those nationally, became more polarized, harsher, and much less courteous. On all sides. Tom sometimes shouted at the mayor, and Margaret lost her temper with Tom. I spoke out of turn when the mayor refused to call on me. Mike even walked out of a couple of meetings because it was late, and he was tired and fed up.

Part of this is not ideological, but rests on the ability of the chair to run the meeting well and keep control. The mayor doesn't keep a firm hand on her gavel. Still, something bigger than tone was shifting. Why does the far right in Haines want to stop funding the library? The pool? The arts center? They threaten to remove the very reasons I love living in this town. Why does the far left question every new tour permit and oppose seasonal vacation rental applications? That prevents people from earning a living so they can afford to live here and use the library and pool and attend one of Tresham's theater productions and grow to love it all as I do.

One strategy for breaking this unhealthy cycle is agreeing to follow some basic rules of conduct, and enforcing them at local meetings, no matter if all the shouting and put-downs are acceptable on TV or Twitter. Placing all of the emotions and personal relationships aside, legislating comes down to actions made through motions, seconds, and votes. I know that sounds like wonky talk, but it's true. Now more than ever it is important to have high standards for civil public engagement. *Robert's Rules* really do contain the debate so time isn't wasted, and, who knows, they may eventually help us paint some buildings. And if you are at all interested in public service, learning the rules of your own municipality or legislative body is a good idea. They will pull you out of the muddy pit where no one is saying anything they haven't already said and everyone is growing angrier and angrier at one another, especially after it dawns on you that you have the majority votes to turn down a proposal for a large timber sale on the Chilkat Peninsula and can end the debate by asking the mayor to please "Call for the Question."

My new favorite somewhat obscure motion usually comes after a decisive moment like that, when I move for a short recess for "A Question of Privilege." This requires no second and allows me to pause the meeting to use the restroom, and for everyone to regroup and take a breather. It's more discreet than saying I have to go to the bathroom. But sometimes when I make this announcement, there is a blank look from the clerk, the mayor, assembly members, and the manager. They may not have read the fine print in the *Idiot's Guide,* so I whisper, "Bathroom break?" and everyone nods with an "Ohhh."

Walking up the stairs and down the long hall to the women's room offers me a minute or two to calm down, stretch my legs, and sometimes to wake up. It's a small, two-stall, windowless cubby at the end of a winding dark corridor. After the timber sale was nixed, I was wedged in the restroom with Madam Mayor and two women who, down in the chambers, had also spoken in support of logging and berated the assembly, including me, as anti-business environmentalists for opposing it. The majority of the assembly disagreed with them and we had just said so collectively by voting "no." Downstairs, the air was thick. I felt the tension up here, too. Yet even without *Robert's Rules* in force, we all minded our tongues. No one gloated or growled. We nodded with half-smiles and whispered "excuse me" as we reached for the paper towels or accidentally bumped into one another. The sounds of tinkling, flushing, and washing hands are so intimate and feminine that for a few minutes anyway, we were all the same. Everything was okay. It was almost like soaking nude in the Tenakee hot spring.

You have no idea how much hope this gave me.

‖‖‖

Manager and Committee Reports

The Parks & Rec committee spoke with State Park Ranger Russell regarding the desirability of an outhouse at Mosquito Lake. He agreed that it is a good idea but not supported by the administration. Further ways to fund an outhouse without state management will be researched. It was also agreed that if an outhouse is installed, there should also be some bear-proof trash cans.

Police estimate the values of the recent drug seizure to be:
• 24 Marijuana seedlings = $24,000
• 14 Mature budding plants = $56,000
• 19 Juvenile plants = $38,000

The Sewer & Water Dept. processed 19,150 lbs. of sludge and treated 7,395,000 gallons of water.

Public Works has been stockpiling sand for winter roads, replaced the doors to the fire hall, and finished prepping and crushing nineteen derelict vehicles to be shipped out on the scrap metal barge.

‖‖‖

★ FOUR ★

It's Problematic

HAINES ISN'T A city. It's a remote rural borough the size of a small state, mostly wild and roadless, with some outlying settlements beyond Haines proper. The townsite is over a hundred years old, with sidewalks and streetlights and a business district and police department, as well as the school, cultural centers, a harbor, and residential areas that extend a few miles in each direction from Main Street. After the Alaska State Trooper who patrolled the rural areas outside of town was reassigned to another part of the state—there was not enough crime to justify the expense—one solution the assembly considered was extending police service from town out along the limited rural road system. At a public hearing to determine if the question should be placed on an upcoming ballot, a gray-haired, rosy-cheeked woman with round glasses and an appliqué sweatshirt said she would not vote for it, because if a burglar tried to break into her house near Mosquito Lake, she certainly wouldn't call 911 and offer him a snack while the two of them waited for a cop to drive the thirty miles to her place. The only thing the police could do for her was "bring me a body bag." She has a gun, she said, and she would use it.

"Wait," said my friend Beth the next morning when I told her about the meeting. I walk with Beth and our dogs every morning on the Chilkat Inlet beach. "Did she really say she'd kill someone. In a public meeting?"

"Yup."

"Is that even legal?"

"It all depends."

"On what?"

"If he shoots first."

"That's not funny," she said.

"But you're laughing."

IT HAS ALWAYS seemed easy to write about this town and the people who live here because there are stories everywhere. I'm not so much creating them as recording them. Almost every day someone or something I witness makes me laugh or cry or thump my forehead and think, *Wow, that's incredible.* Einstein observed that we humans are all dependent on the invisible labors of others. I think he meant that the computer I type on was designed by a Silicon Valley wizard and that my underwear was sewn by a stranger in Malaysia (if, that is, Einstein could have imagined such particulars back then). These ties to our well-being are more obvious closer to home. I know the people who fix my boiler, sell me groceries, teach my grandchildren, and plow the roads, and they know me and my family. Some are friends, some not, but they make my life healthier, safer, easier, and infinitely more entertaining.

My own work depends on these residents, as much as Chip's lumberyard does. They are the inspiration for my writing. If I had not more or less randomly arrived in Haines when I was twenty-four with Chip and our oldest daughter, Eliza, then a baby, would I even be a writer? I don't know. Here's an unexpected connection: the woman at the meeting last night, the one who said that she was prepared to shoot to kill (and I don't doubt her), is a fan of my books and had followed my blog from a distance, which was part of the reason why she and her husband chose to retire to Haines from the Midwest. They drive into town for just about every assembly meeting, and their interest in politics has nothing to do with me. She probably prefers my author self to my meeting self.

Michel de Montaigne may have been the first writer who wrote about his experiences using "I" in such a way that readers learned something valuable about themselves—and he did it in the roundabout style of discovery and doubt that is now known as the personal essay. He was also the mayor of Bordeaux for four years in the 1580s. He kept writing, though, and was vigilant about protecting his creative and personal life. Montaigne was by all accounts a good mayor but, surely, he stared down critics and struggled with decisions. How did he keep his mayoral duties from consuming all his time and energy? "Lend yourself to others, but only give yourself to yourself," he wrote.

So what do I do about Ports and Harbors Committee member Big Don? I can still see him, with a his blue construction company cap above a trimmed beard, no mustache, like an Amish farmer, his arms crossed and scowling at me during the awful meeting on the harbor expansion project that took place about two weeks after I was elected. That was around the same time he first brought up the threat of circulating a petition to hold a recall election to remove at least three of the assembly members for misconduct in office, myself included. The recall process takes months. In the meantime, getting me off the assembly one way or another seemed to be his new mission in life. It was disappointing since I had always believed he was a gentle giant, a teddy bear of a man, annoying but essentially kind.

Big Don had been a frequent visitor to my kitchen for years. During my tenure on the Haines Planning Commission a few years back he would stand at our kitchen island made out of a workbench from the lumberyard and share his perspective about zoning or planning matters. His views were usually different from mine. Big Don did not want a small park on the corner of Main Street and Third Avenue. He did not want the library to build an addition. He did not want noise restrictions on the type of brakes dump trucks can use. Even before that, when I was on the school board and the new school was being planned, he came to all our meetings with plenty of advice on its design and construction. Some of it was good. Sometimes we even agreed.

Eventually I ended up encouraging him to call first before stopping by the house because I had work to do and deadlines to meet. I'd pick up the phone, and he'd say, "Do you have a minute?"

I'd look at the obituary or column or draft of an essay I was working on and say, "Well, I'm busy but if you make it quick . . ."

"I'll be right there," he'd say, and hang up before I could squeak, "No, I meant we can talk on the phone, I am not even dressed yet and I've been up since four and need another hour to finish this."

Don is retired from his family's contracting company—they dig septic systems, clear land, and prepare building sites—so he's got some time on his hands. A few minutes after the call he would pull into our driveway (which he built, as he had most of the driveways on Mud Bay Road), step onto the back porch, wave at me through the kitchen window, and walk in. At least my pajamas are heavy flannel.

"Coffee?"

"Sure if you got some made," he'd say.

Big Don and I had been at odds over the harbor design from the beginning, back when I was first on the planning commission and opposed it. I wanted it to be beautiful and practical. He just wanted practical, but even then, it wasn't. There were not enough new slips for the boats on the waiting list. There were none actually. They would apparently come when another ten million or so dollars materialized from . . . where? But that didn't prevent him from trying to influence me. I really didn't like the proposed four-acre parking lot that had me humming Joni Mitchell's song about paving paradise, or adding a six-hundred-foot-long industrial steel wave barrier wall to the picture-postcard view of the docks, fishing boats, rock breakwater, and the blue-green fjord with the snow-capped mountains on the other side.

I suspect he thought I was dumb as a post to not understand why heavy-duty trucks like his, the ones that pull cabin cruiser trailers, need lots of room to park. He did allow that the steel wall was "going to be ugly."

"I'm not going to lie to you," Big Don told me, but he believed it to be the best option.

EARLY ONE SATURDAY morning the summer before I became a candidate for the assembly, I returned up the beach path from walking with Beth. Chip was tuning his bike and nodded toward Don's pickup truck idling by the woodshed. "Your new best friend is here," Chip said. He frowned. We had planned a long bike ride before babysitting a couple of granddaughters in the afternoon. "We're leaving in fifteen minutes," he reminded me under his breath and went inside to change.

Big Don walked toward me with a roll of the harbor drawings under his arm. I said I hoped he knew he wasn't going to change my mind. He smiled and said it wouldn't hurt to try and could I look at these a moment with him? I explained that it was not a good time and, actually, there wouldn't ever be one because I don't like the design that you do, so let's agree to drop the subject, okay? Besides, I have an appointment in fifteen minutes. (If I'd said I was going on a bike ride, he might get really mad, or stay, figuring that wasn't as important as his concerns.) He looked as frustrated as I felt.

Who knows why, maybe it's a congenital heart defect, but I felt bad for him. Part of me also wanted to prove to Don that I am more intelligent and capable than he gave me credit for, and do not have rocks for brains. I told him to wait a second, ran in the house, and came back with my latest book, *Find the Good*. "For you," I said. "It's a present." I signed it for him.

DURING MY CAMPAIGN, even though I knew he would never vote for me—Don actively touted the two most conservative candidates (who lost to Tom and me) even though one had a history of domestic violence—I was still shocked when Big Don placed an ad in the last paper to come out before the election urging voters not to vote for Tom or me because we were "aligned with the Mud Bay liberal types" (printed in bold letters) and that "the silent majority" needs to "get off the couch and vote if you don't want the liberal Mud Bay types running our borough."

There were more accusations, too, but no time to refute any of his claims publicly before Election Day. I was so upset that I called my daughter Sarah, who lives across town with her husband and two of my grandchildren, Caroline and Ivy. "It's basically true, Mom," she said. "You are against the boat harbor project and you like the library and parks, so don't worry about it. That's why people will vote for you."

Sarah is so smart.

A few days before the ad was printed, while standing in my kitchen, Big Don let go of the harbor debate and now wanted to know how I felt about a future local Get Out the Vote campaign. It was too late for this year, he said, but it could begin soon for the next election cycle. He feared that the "wrong people" win elections because "the right people" don't vote. His own granddaughter, a college student, wasn't even registered, he said. I told him I thought the high school should help to register every student to vote when they reach eighteen, and mail out voter registration forms after graduation to the rest.

"You'd support that?" he asked.

"Of course I would."

"Well, we agree on something."

I thought my hospitality mattered. I thought that Don and I had an unspoken agreement to be decent to each other. Yes, he could place an ad for another candidate, but to lash out against me and a whole group of my neighbors by calling us "Mud Bay types" was wrong. There's something rotten about that line of thinking and it is becoming more and more acceptable. Broad brushes are for applying paint to fences, not labeling people as all the same because of where they live. Again I wonder about Trump's influence. Especially when Big Don started talking more seriously about taking the town back by recalling the liberal, incompetent, anti-economic development and potentially illegally acting members of the assembly, and when he reminded his supporters to use social media as a source for assembly news and comments and ignore newspaper and radio reports.

But maybe the vitriol is not so new, and Trump has only encouraged the worst instincts in otherwise decent people, under the guise of praising straight talkers. It's possible that I had ignored the simmering anger in Haines that is the flip side of our progressive community's activism. The divide between the so-called loggers and hippies can be deep and always has been, even if the "hippies" now have beautiful homes and work hard and the "loggers" are now miners or fishermen or retired cops from Michigan.

My elderly neighbor Betty considers herself conservative. She thinks people on welfare should be required to work, she never drinks or smokes, and the gun in her linen closet is loaded. When I picked up the phone the day after Don's ad ran, instead of "hello" Betty said, "Am I one of those 'Mud Bay hippies' now?" and laughed. Betty and Big Don are old friends. Since her husband died, he helps her with picking apples or hammering in the snowplow guide sticks along her driveway. He always brings her his home-smoked salmon.

Betty voted for me but has never attended an assembly meeting, and I doubt that she even discussed my election with Don. For my views on the harbor and the mine, five hundred people chose me over Don's candidates, including Betty, which might surprise

Don. But, like her, most residents don't have the time or inclination to spend evenings in long, sometimes boring meetings. The retired schoolteachers who supported me, for example, and my own campaign manager, Teresa, stay as far away from assembly meetings as possible. I don't think Teresa has actually *ever* been to one. Chip hasn't, either. Not since he served in local government about twenty years ago. Sarah came when preschool funding was on the agenda with the other preschool parents. Beth was at one about a correction to her property lines.

I shouldn't say my supporters never show up, though. Some do. Like Pizza Joe, the artist who rollerblades around town in a brown bear suit, and the gas station owner with the US Constitution booklet in his pocket who threatens to sue the borough for violating his rights (and when he does, succeeds), or the tie-dyed conspiracy theorist who offered the assembly free marijuana samples.

"During a meeting?" Beth asked as we walked the next day.

"Yup." I can't make this kind of stuff up.

He had explained, correctly, that it was legal to possess and give pot away (soon it would be legal to sell, with a license from the state of the Alaska) and then said how much he appreciated my friendship. I am apparently the only person who doesn't hang up when he calls to complain about the police department harassing him for suspicious behavior.

IT IS STILL amazing to me that the official public record of my second assembly meeting, on All Saint's Day 2016, is only a page and a half long and reveals nothing that would lead a casual reader to understand why it affected my life in this community so strongly, and why it continues to resonate. The issue was straightforward. Should we have a public vote on accepting the harbor project? If we agreed to do that, then there would be a special election as soon as possible, not to hold it up in case it passed. I thought it was reasonable to ask residents whether they approved of the preferred design of the largest municipal project in our history before awarding the construction contract. I had promised to support this referendum when I campaigned.

Haines is a waterfront town, and access to beaches and the views of the inlets are valued by residents and visitors alike. The cruise ship dock near the small boat harbor had recently been expanded and rebuilt. A large paved parking lot with bathrooms had been constructed on a bulkhead jutting onto a popular beach, and around the point the ferry terminal parking lot had been greatly expanded on another large waterfront lot—and now a new beachfront development was proposed that would further alter the feeling and look of the town in a significant way. People were divided over it and remain so. Of course supporting fishermen was important, but not at all costs to everyone else.

There were plenty of passionate displays on both sides of the issue, including an Independence Day Parade float disparaging the steel wall and an ad in the paper that photoshopped a 747 onto the proposed parking lot, with room to spare. The arguments were intense. The Haines Borough manager at the time even asked the police to bar two critics from a planning meeting in the library. One of them was the constitution guy, and the assembly later issued a public apology and he agreed not to sue us that time.

The day before the meeting I bumped into the husband of my fellow assembly member Margaret on the beach. John is a photographer whose images hang in art galleries throughout Alaska and who also captains the fishing boat his father worked on before him. Whenever we see each other across the tide flats we usually catch up or wait and walk together and talk. That's how I know that his grandmother was a survivor of a Spanish flu epidemic that killed all but three babies in her Alaska Native village of about two thousand souls. Relatives far from that place adopted her. I can't imagine the grief. Two thousand dead? That's our whole town.

"I'm just grateful that I inherited her immune system. I never get sick," John had told me. I wondered if he celebrated Thanksgiving. Indigenous People's Day has replaced Columbus Day in Alaska, and I'd heard that some Alaska Natives don't do Thanksgiving dinner. "It's problematic," John said, because he likes the turkey and Margaret bakes great desserts and, he paused, looking around at the view we both love, there is so much to be thankful for. Here's something I didn't say that day, but I wished I had: why did we assume that Thanksgiving is only problematic for Native people? When will people like me, whose English ancestors were responsible for introducing deadly germs, and caused more death and destruction than the flu of 1919, question our version of American history?

When we parted on that day before my fateful second assembly meeting, I promised to bring John's dog's ball to the meeting and give it to Margaret. I knew that John, like Margaret, disagreed with me on the harbor. I wished Pearl had dropped Buddy's tennis ball when I asked her to. I wish she hadn't stolen it, then of all times.

In the big meeting, when John spoke against holding a special election on the harbor, he was polite and courteous. He said it was time to move forward and too late to change direction. If only my chair were not so close to the public microphone, though. Sitting near to him made it even harder to let him—and Margaret—down.

Then another fisherman stood up—Stuart, whom I coached on the high school cross country team and is one of Sarah's best friends (he married Sarah's college roommate after falling in love with her when she visited us in Haines and now they have three little children). He looked right at me and said the assembly decision to even consider the special election made him feel like he was "getting slapped in the face." His voice broke when he said the lack of support for fishermen it demonstrated was killing him because he had "so much invested in this community." Stuart expected more, he muttered, especially from me, and then his face crumpled and he walked out.

I wanted to assure him there could be a better way, one that would help him more. This is why I don't believe that line from *Love Story*: "Love means never having to say you're sorry." I love this town because I care about a lot of the people who live here, very much. I deeply love a lot of them, and that's why I'm always saying I'm sorry. Montaigne may have survived as a mayor as well as a writer for as long as he did because he understood that in public life, especially, "there are no truths, only moments of clarity passing for answers."

Don's preferred harbor plan gave him a new ramp for his cabin cruiser but it did not add one additional slip or dock, not even the drive-on pier that Stuart and John both said they needed in order to move heavy nets and gear to and from their boat decks more safely than the funky old hoist could. But by then the momentum of the testimony was against the special election for the referendum I had campaigned on. Somehow, the whole harbor issue had become black and white, yes or no, with fishermen or against them. My son and son-in-law were fishermen, yet I was the enemy. I don't know how that happened, but it happens a lot in politics.

Camps are pitched and battle lines drawn. Look at Brexit. Look at the border with Mexico. There were a lot of reasonable concerns somewhere in the middle between the UK leaving or staying in the EU, and the humanitarian crisis at the border and a wall.

Don hadn't changed my mind, and I wasn't going to change anyone's tonight. Too bad we couldn't cut the meeting short and lessen the pain. But that was not in the rule book. Public hearings are, though, and who would want to restrict the people's right to speak? Almost all those present testified against the vote, and almost all were furious about it. The husband of a woman I volunteer with on the hospice board looked like he wanted to punch someone. He said that the timing of the vote—it would have been in December—would mean many fishermen, who take their vacations in the winter, wouldn't be here. "That smells," he said. "That really smells." Did he really believe that those of us who wanted the harbor design choice election were that conniving? Truth is, we had already tried to explain that it *had* to happen soon, in order not to slow up the project if people voted for it.

The chairman of the planning commission, a ponytailed artist who lives on Mud Bay Road, asked what would happen if the majority didn't vote for the chosen design? "Go back to the drawing board?" That's impossible, he said, it's too late now. All I could think was, *Then why had this question been pivotal to my election and to Tom's if it was already moot?* Is this what happens in national campaigns, too? Are candidates chosen by voters based on hot button issues that are not actually up for debate by the time they are sworn in?

I couldn't believe it when Tom raised his voice and said, "I have driven drunk and I have woken up in the wrong house, but if I'm asked to spend $15 or $30 million of other people's money on something they don't want, it will be by far the most reckless thing I've done." I knew he meant well, and he was already the most quoted of the assembly members by the media and would continue to be, but he certainly wasn't always the most helpful. Many meetings later, during a debate over new guidelines for backyard pet burials, Tom said he would vote for them, which would have been fine, but then he added that this does raise the question in his mind of why we prohibit the burial of human bodies at home. "Conceivably," Tom said, "you could bury a giant malamute here that's twice the size of an infant on your property." He did not see me put my head on the desk or the look of horror from the president of the Chamber of Commerce, a mother of two children.

Now, listening to testimony on the harbor vote, my heart was beating oddly and I was afraid of something I couldn't name. Was that heart defect I feared I may have a leaky valve? Or only a murmur? One of the symptoms of an impending heart attack is this profound sense of dread.

In the end, I did not need CPR, even though my side lost. The clerk's minutes name the staff and visitors who testified for and against the resolution and note that it failed by an assembly vote of 4–3 when the mayor broke the tie. There would be no public vote. The harbor would be built according to the same plans that Don favored and lobbied for in my kitchen.

A FEW DAYS after the meeting I saw John on the beach again. We walked toward each other, and then together for a bit. I asked how his latest exhibit was coming; he said the matting and framing was tedious. He asked how the television show based on my books was going; I'd been in the news because an English company planned to produce a semi-fictional drama based on my work, which is, of course, my life. I said, "Okay, but so far, the writers want us to own a bar instead of a lumberyard, one of our children to be transgender, and the Chip character might be a ghost."

"What?"

"Maybe they think there's not enough drama around here?" I said.

"Guess they've never been to an assembly meeting."

John threw a ball for Buddy before I could stop him or grab Pearl's collar. She always beats Buddy to the ball and then refuses to drop it. John sometimes forgets this. "Oh no," he said, too late. He never seems to mind Pearl's bad manners as much as I do. He shrugged, said not to worry about it, and a few steps later, more quietly said that he was glad the harbor was finally being expanded, but that he was sorry that the process "hadn't been the best." I said I hoped I was wrong, and that the wall wouldn't look too bad and that we'd find the money for the docks and slips.

The fellow hospice board member whose husband was so mad at me still greets me with a smiling hello in the pool locker room, but she keeps the conversation to safe subjects like last night's snowfall and tomorrow's brighter forecast. I can't assure her that it's just politics, not real life, and there's no hard feelings, because I am privately holding some anger about it all, too.

I saw Stuart up at Sarah's house and we watched a football game together in my son-in-law's basement sports bar for a few minutes before I went back upstairs with the mothers and children. I pretended it wasn't awkward. He did, too, and handed me a beer, and we talked about his trapline and the time he took me with him on the back of a four-wheeler to check for marten. "That was a while ago," he said.

He was a bachelor then; now he was a dad. I used to be his favorite coach when he ran on the cross country team in high school. "A lifetime ago," I said.

"No kidding," he said.

DID I TELL you that the day after I gave him my book, Big Don returned to my house? He didn't stay long enough to turn off his truck, and he didn't even mention politics. He said he had been up all night reading. The chapter about his friend Pete Lapham's life and death was his favorite. Pete was Diana's husband. The same Diana I had defeated and who called Tom despicable. The same Diana whose husband's eulogy I wrote and delivered at his funeral. I really liked Pete. She really loved him.

"I have to admit," Don said to me, in what would be one of our last amicable conversations, "you even made me a little teary. It's darn good."

"Thank you," I said. "That means a lot."

Yes, John, I also have a lot to be thankful for in spite of myself, and, yes, you are right: it is problematic.

Manager and Committee Reports

Preconstruction meetings for the harbor expansion were held.

For the eighth year in a row the Haines Borough Public Library has been designated a Star Library by *Library Journal* based on our high circulation, program attendance, and internet use per capita.

The Tourism Director is working on solutions to the lack of cab or shuttle service from the ferry terminal or airport to town.

The Lands Department's data collection crew for property tax assessments is working in the field three days a week. Henry and Scott make an excellent team with extremely positive attitudes and are unfazed by the winter weather.

FIVE

Lessons in Civility

I'VE TAPED MARY Oliver's poem "Praying" to my desk for inspiration. She writes that "It," which I read as life, writing, my work on the assembly—all of it—"isn't a contest but the doorway into thanks" and that it is entered through silence, which allows a different and, I would assume kinder, voice to speak. Near the poem is a Virgin Mary devotional candle I bought in Mexico, a string of miniature Buddhist prayer flags from my friend Stephanie, and a long, narrow, framed turn-of-the-millennium portrait of the citizens of Haines taken in May 1999 on the Fort Seward parade grounds. Stephanie also gave me the coffee-stained paperback now filled with my sticky notes, *Choosing Civility: The Twenty-Five Rules of Considerate Conduct* by P. M. Forni.

Stephanie is a former mayor of Haines. I leaned on her wisdom when I needed advice before the first few assembly meetings, and have ever since. I know what you're thinking: *another* former mayor? So far there's Jerry, also a former assemblyman and whom Tresham defeated; Mike who is still on the assembly; and now Stephanie. The current mayor is a former mayor, too, as she was mayor before Stephanie was, and then defeated Stephanie to become the mayor again when Stephanie's term was up. Yes, turnover is high but at least we pay attention and when we don't like something, we do something about it. In Haines, if you complain too much about anything, from the decorations at the high school prom to the timing of the annual spring trash cleanup, then you will be invited to organize it the following year. Likewise, if you don't like the town's leadership, you run for office, or put your name in for a committee appointment.

Stephanie grew up Quaker in Philadelphia. She arrived in Haines as a young woman with her former husband, and they set up a yurt on a cove called Paradise, grew a garden, and had three children. I think she was our first La Leche Leaguer. I know she was the borough clerk in the 1970s, a special education teacher, and now is a flower farmer and a part-time caregiver for a young disabled woman. When Stephanie arrives with my bouquet— she delivers them weekly to her subscribers and calls herself the Flower Fairy—we always talk political philosophy. Not so much the issues, as how to tackle them effectively. She has been a huge help. Once, when I told her that the tension at the meetings about nearly everything and the recall threats, too, were getting to me, how it was so thick I could practically taste it the minute I walked into a meeting, she told me, "Pretend you are in your house, and you are the host." When she was mayor, she said, she imagined the assembly chambers as her living room and everyone in it as her guests. When she gave me *Choosing Civility,* it was already battered and full of starred pages and margin notes. She had underlined phrases like "civility belongs in the realm of ethics" and being civil requires "constantly being aware of others" and seeking ways to be respectful and considerate. I'm a little too constantly aware of others, but perhaps that can be a good thing?

Like Stephanie, I attended a Quaker school. My family was Episcopalian, but my mother taught Spanish and was a principal there. It was easy to appreciate the values of the Religious Society of Friends. All these years later, I still remember their tenets and how my teachers admired them. Quakers spend a lot of time in quiet reflection, and during Quaker Meeting or any public forum they only speak, as they say, when "the spirit moves them." They also believe that "there is that of God in every man" and the quiet voice inside that calls them to action is divine. In Quaker Meeting, when Quakers hear that spirit voice, they stand, comment, and sit back down. There is no conversation or debate. If one person's thoughts nudge another's spirit to rise, they may speak but not rebuke or praise the previous speaker. They seek consensus.

We are not all Quakers, or even, as my mother and the rest of the faculty at Friends Academy used to say, "similarly senti-mented." At a meeting before construction on the Haines harbor began, I asked a question about what effect extending the waste-water treatment plant outfall line farther into the cove might have on water quality, and especially on the fish we eat. A fisher-man and member of the harbor committee answered me by saying that the biggest, "juiciest" crabs he catches come from directly in front of that sewer pipe, and he saves those to sell to his "Democratic customers," like me, and he chuckled and his buddies did, too.

If the chambers was my living room, and he was my guest, would he still speak to me that way? Would anyone?

Part of the problem could be physical. The assembly cham-bers is about as charming as the waiting room of a juvenile deten-tion facility. The fluorescent lighting makes everyone look ill and the poor ventilation will probably make us sick, thanks to that phlegmy rattle of a cougher who sometimes sits in the back row or the standing water in the crawlspace beneath us. Fresh paint would help, as would local artwork. The ceiling is too low. Spending tax dollars on interior decorating would cause Big Don even more heartburn than when I added those landscaping funds to beautify that big new harbor parking lot. He's still steaming about my shrubberies and they haven't even been planted yet. Of course, there are other ways to make people comfortable in a sitting room than to remodel. Heat. Courteous hosts. Gin.

THE FIRST TIME that Chip and I sat down to dinner alone, after our youngest daughter went off to college, there was a long pause. Do we still hold hands and say grace? I had continued my parents' tradition of giving thanks before dinner with my own children and added a new twist, which made my stiff-upper-lip mother quaff her wine and caused my dad to remark, "What's with the hand-holding?"

Chip and I did say grace that first night alone, shyly. It's not as if we're as Jesus-y as Rosalynn and Jimmy Carter, but saying it felt important, and still does. I have taught our grandchildren to hold hands and say, "For all that we have and are about to receive make us truly grateful and keep us mindful of the needs of others. Amen." When you ask out loud for help in being more considerate, you just might be, and when you aren't, at least you'll be aware that you should keep trying. That's why I'm working on not saying what I really think, especially when I'm angry. Instead, as I drive home, I have imaginary exchanges with some of these guys who are so rude. Then I let them have it. I am witty and sharp and brave. It helps that I can talk to Beth privately, discreetly, outside where no one can hear me except our dogs and the crows.

"Can you believe that son of a bitch said that? He might as well have told me to eat shit," I shouted into the wind as I told the story of the crappy crabber. "Seriously? I couldn't believe it when he said that about the sewer pipe, and no one called him on it. Not a one! It was all I could do not to scream and walk out. What the hell?"

I am swearing way too much lately.

"Why didn't you?" asked Beth.

"I don't know. Maybe I was afraid to? And what good would it do? He says stuff like that because he wants a fight. If I don't take his 'bait' and don't yell back, then it can't escalate. There's a reason silence is golden."

"It's funny though."

"What?"

"Crappy crabs."

"I can't even eat crab. I'm allergic to it."

"Did you say that?"

"No."

But it did make me feel better knowing that I could have, and it would have been a great comeback and made everyone laugh. I would like to think I kept quiet because I am wise. I do agree with Michelle Obama when she advised to go high when critics go low, and you can't sink much lower than selling crabs caught feeding on effluent from the sewer pipe. In truth, though, I may not be fearless enough to confront bullies in public.

BEFORE WE GO too much further with this story, you need to understand that Haines Borough has what is called a manager form of government, which means the manager is hired by the assembly to run the town's day-to-day business and supervise employees, but the assembly sets the policies that guide the manager. (By the way, assembly members receive an honorarium of $3,500 a year; the mayor earns about twice that. Now. More on that later.) The job of the mayor is to preside over meetings and give a report to the assembly in which she may or may not offer advice (that the assembly may or may not take). The mayor also appoints members of committees, boards, and commissions; however, the assembly must approve them. The mayor only votes in case of a tie. The manager serves at the assembly's pleasure. Like assembly members, the mayor is elected to a three-year term; that the seats are up for election at different times is both negative and positive.

This system can work great if everyone is respectful and supportive of one another's roles. Professionally trained public administrators, i.e., our borough manager, should be better equipped to run a municipality than amateurs like me. The manager is to the government what the superintendent is to the school district. The mayor and the assembly don't have to agree on anything, except for the way we speak to one another, although I suppose the mayor has the final word on that, and a gavel to enforce it. Ideally, the mayor makes appointments that don't conflict with the assembly's values.

The setup can also be a recipe for instability. If, for instance, a newly elected assembly member joins three other assembly members who already disagree with a recent manager decision regarding, say, the police department or the pool hours, and if the manager ignores the assembly's direction or chooses not to take much of it for long enough, the most likely options are either for the assembly to find a new manager or for the manager to seek work elsewhere.

Most of our borough managers have come from other places, because not many locals have the expertise for the job. Or at least we don't all believe they do. It's hard to be a prophet in your hometown. Jesus couldn't even pull it off. The first borough manager I worked with on the assembly (there would be three in my three years) was fired late one evening on the heels of the harbor decision after a longer than usual break between meetings in which tensions had grown. I blame some of what happened next on the weather.

The manager had arrived in Haines from Florida the previous June. It had been a mild fall and the first major snowstorm didn't blow in until November 29. A former Coast Guard officer, the still-relatively-new manager took the storm warnings seriously and canceled the assembly meeting scheduled for that night. It may have been the first time in history that a meeting was canceled because of bad weather. I'm not sure the manager ever got past that overreaction.

Northern people dwell in winter. My porch and mudroom reflect that way of life. Outside are the shovel, firewood, ax, and the kindling bin. Inside, waterproof coats and pants as well as down, wool, and fleece jackets; rubber boots and insulated boots, ice grippers and snowshoes. On the shelf sit headlamps for walking the dog in the dark and an LED lantern for my granddaughters to light their way back home—their mother, our daughter Stoli, and her family live next door—on dark winter afternoons when there are only about six hours of daylight. Even when it's snowing sideways and wind chills are well below zero, the kids go to school and Beth and I walk. The dogs don't mind the cold, but we wrap our faces in scarves and balaclavas. I have skied to play rehearsals and surfed my Subaru through a blizzard to the annual holiday lighting of the library Christmas tree, arriving to find the library full of elders with canes and young mothers with babies, all congratulating one another for not letting a little weather spoil our party.

National Weather Service forecasters in Juneau predicted this storm with the usual alarming hyperbole that heavy snow and wind would make driving hazardous and pose a "potential risk to life and property." It must be a legal requirement, although I don't think you can sue the weather service. If that were possible someone around here would have tried it by now. When the manager and the police chief, who had also only just moved to Haines—he was from the Washington, DC, area—received the weather alert over their new, improved emergency warning system, they closed the borough office and the library and told everyone to go home. They put an announcement on the radio asking residents to stay indoors and shelter in place until the storm passed, as if it were a Category 4 hurricane.

I heard the message in the car, while swerving in the slushy ruts on my way up Cemetery Hill to town for groceries. I haven't subscribed to the new borough-wide alert system for my cell phone because I have spotty cell service at my house anyway, and rely on my neighbor Betty to call me about anything unusual in the forecast or on our road, for that matter. The snow was mixed with rain by then. I wished it were colder so it would stick. I was hoping for a white Christmas, and there should be snow on the ground by now. "Winter is not an emergency," I said to the radio, and to the dog riding shotgun. "We can't stay home until spring, can we, Pearl?" The precipitation was all rain by evening, which made the over-the-top response even more embarrassing. I received a few phone complaints and snarky emails about it as well as taking some good-natured ribbing at a holiday craft bazaar.

When we finally did convene on December 16 for the last meeting of that year, there was a lot on the agenda, enough for two meetings because of the one we missed, including the manager's evaluation. Since the manager serves at our will, and relations had been rocky well before the alarmist hoopla during the storm, I figured he knew it was possible that he might not be asked to continue. In fact, we had all delivered written evaluations of his job performance to the mayor two weeks earlier and most of the assembly assumed she had shown these to the manager. I know I did. But apparently he had not seen them before the meeting. Except for the mayor's evaluation—she was his champion—and Mike's, which was tepid, they were all damning.

Talk about awkward.

The manager had insisted his evaluation be conducted in public, in front of his wife and friends like Diana and Big Don and the police chief and his wife, and all residents in attendance. We had suggested it be private but he declined the offer, thinking, I suppose, that we would be more forgiving in public. And so began an extremely uncomfortable session that was nothing like an evening with guests in my living room. What was Stephanie talking about? Was she speaking figuratively and I took it literally? I am not sure there even *is* a living room in her cozy farmhouse. I've never been beyond the garden deck and her warm kitchen/sitting room. And now that I think about it, she does eat a lot of her meals at Beth's, and celebrates holidays there, too.

Assemblywoman Friedenauer was soft-spoken though firm, as she explained her concerns, which were many and incorporated all of mine as well, from his lack of basic knowledge of borough government to missteps, some serious, with employees, assembly members, and residents. She asked him how he thought he could remedy the situation and he responded that he wanted to work with us but offered no specifics.

Assemblymen Jackson and Gregg spoke of liking him personally and that they had hoped their experiment to hire a manager without any municipal experience would have worked, but it hadn't. Those three had been on the assembly that hired him and led the charge. They also acknowledged some of the blame for not providing him with more training and direction. Mike was quiet. Tom and I were brand new.

The manager did not seem to understand the gravity of his situation or give the assembly any way to help him out of it. His solution for improving communication was basically "come to my office and talk to me," even though he had just learned from the evaluations that some of us on the assembly felt that he often said one thing to one person and another thing to someone else, ensuring we all heard what we wanted to hear. Also, assembly members weren't all that welcome in his office, at least not this one. To me, it felt more like the den of a men's club. Big Don and the police chief might as well have had recliners in there.

Then Assemblyman Tom Morphet lost patience. Never one to sugarcoat his words, he roared that the manager was the highest paid person in the borough government and, at about $100,000 annually, those weren't training wages, folks, and furthermore they were public dollars, the people's hard-earned dough. And then Tom read a litany of charges against the manager, largely based on his previous reporting (before he was elected) on the borough administration for the *Chilkat Valley News*.

Assemblyman Mike Case made a motion to place the manager on probation for ninety days. There was a pause, and I seconded it. The other assembly members were surprised, especially since my evaluation of the manager had been bad. I had documented pages of reasons why I believed he wasn't a good fit for Haines. It was no secret that I was not a fan and hadn't been before I took office. His answers tonight had not changed my mind, but his demeanor had, as had the public comments. He appeared to have been blindsided and I thought this public shaming was wrong. We should treat people the way we want to be treated, and that ethic guided my vote to second Assemblyman Case's motion. In my years of involvement in this town, I had been part of organizations, nonprofits, even the school board, in which I had helped end someone's job with a zeal equal to Tom's, and forced them out in a manner that I look back on now as unfair and unkind. I don't regret the outcomes, but I do regret the methods. Also, it was Christmastime, as one of the manager's few defenders had noted. How could we fire a person at Christmas? I have practically memorized *A Christmas Carol*. The chains we forge in life and all of that.

My thinking was that the ninety-day probation would go quickly and not change the final result. He may even choose to resign since obviously we weren't a good fit for him, either. The probation time would ease the transition to a new manager. But Mike and I did not prevail. After the assembly voted 4–2 to fire the manager, there was a gasp, and someone swore. I felt sick. The mayor, who had at first leaned back in her chair, shot forward, shocked, and then furious. She berated us as a bunch of ax throwers and worse. Clerk Julie cried and muttered that we had no idea what we had just done, and Mike said he was tired, pulled on his coat and navy veteran cap, and walked out.

Which was against the rules. We hadn't adjourned.

THE NEXT DAY a friend congratulated me for my courage in "pulling the trigger" and I had to tell him that, actually, I hadn't. On the flip side, I also spoke with a borough employee who was hurt and angry that I had shown the manager more respect than I had given her—she had revealed to me that he'd made negative comments to staff in her department about her. Did I care so little for her feelings that I'd force her to put up with him for three more months? Did her Christmas matter less than his? The manager had also tried to have a friend of mine fired from a private firm. Did I think that was okay? My friend asked me when he called, and then said that I might not have what it takes to be on the assembly and make the tough decisions.

It really didn't matter how I had voted. Unlike the Supreme Court, there's no dissenting opinion issued. When the assembly takes an action, it becomes the borough's ruling. I had fired the manager. We all had.

Overnight it seemed fliers appeared under windshield wipers on cars and trucks parked on Main Street. I pulled one of them off and saw that it was a cartoon depicting the assembly as the Grinches who stole Christmas. "Did you see the latest?" Margaret, aka Assemblywoman Friedenauer, asked when I answered the phone. She was very upset by the fliers. I was, too, but I apologized for not backing her up at the meeting, and she accepted it. Twice now we had differed. First the harbor, now this. It was the hardest thing she had done on the assembly, she said. I said I hoped the holiday break would allow everyone to calm down, and she reminded me about the beer money for the borough party. Since the manager had planned to buy it, Margaret figured it would be a nice gesture for assembly members to personally pick up the tab at the brewery. So we did.

It didn't help.

I had underestimated how much political decisions affect the lives of the borough employees—those who keep the town running no matter who is in charge. These public servants would rather have a bad manager than none, preferring stability over the latest assembly's idea of perfection. There are Haines Borough employees who have been in the business office, Public Works, and the library for decades, and the town is the better for their dedication. The assembly is lucky to have anyone serve more than one term. By Christmas the following year, two people currently on the assembly will have quit after less than three years' time.

There was a funny moment right after the manager had been fired, in that flash before the boom, when I realized we had no idea what happens next. No one did. Who was in charge of the borough? There was that same kind of nervous laughter that happens in funeral parlors. After the mayor had slept on it, she announced that the clerk would fill in, but only for a few weeks, so we needed to come up with a plan, quickly. When Julie called in sick almost immediately, I knew she wasn't going to save us. An interim manager would be best, followed by a search for a permanent one, or as permanent as possible.

A retired Juneau city manager was interested in taking the interim manager job until May. He said he could give us six months of his time to help stabilize the situation, but that he did not want the permanent position. He'd managed Alaska's capital city to good reviews for ten years and he was local enough, thanks to a recreational cabin at Chilkat Lake and close friends in town, to subscribe to the paper but not so local that his name was ever in it. This seemed like the best solution to me. I could use that time to learn from him—we all could—and his expertise and neutrality would carry us through the winter, when even in good years there are horrible public arguments. This is where those weather warnings are accurate: the cold dark days without much to do are the time when coffee shop and barstool, and now social media chat, do pose a real threat to life, liberty, and the pursuit of happiness for those of us in public office. Cabin fever needs an outlet, and there's nothing like politics to release pent-up anger.

Brad Ryan, our current facilities director, also wanted the position of interim manager now, with an eye toward becoming the permanent one eventually. That would require advertising and interviews, and time. He said he was tired of teaching new managers all about Haines and tired of filling in for them after they left. He had been the interim manager before the guy we just fired but had not applied for the manager's job then, reckoning that, with a young family, the hours were too long. Now, he said, he might as well do it himself to avoid another disaster. Brad has a PhD in biology and is a popular guy. So is his easy-going, good-humored, and capable wife, who works at the library, speaks Polish, and is a friend of my daughter Sarah. The Ryan kids and Sarah's kids play together all the time. I won't presume to have read Brad's mind, but after the vote to fire the manager he looked astounded, and then disgusted. I could understand. There had been a string of managers over the last few years who had come and gone for all kinds of reasons, personal and political, leaving Brad and the other department heads to pick up the slack.

Even so, I thought I could bring Brad around to my view and arranged to meet him in his office in the fire hall. I whistled "Walking in a Winter Wonderland" as I took the stairs two at a time. I was confident that hiring the retired Juneau manager would save the day. Brad nodded and listened while I made my pitch, including how Brad could learn the job from him. I said he would basically train Brad for the permanent position, and the assembly would also benefit as we'd all learn to be better at our jobs by observing this experienced manager. I asked Brad to call him and, if after talking with him, he agreed with me—as I was certain he would—then Brad could make the hiring suggestion himself at the next assembly meeting. That way we'd show unity and probably would all agree on this course of action. Even the mayor. I left the fire hall feeling lighter, and like a statesman. I was learning how to make positive changes. Maybe I'm good at this assembly thing after all, I thought.

I should have looked up and seen the safe about to fall on my head.

A FEW DAYS before Christmas, still proud of myself, I listened to the slush and wind strafe the house and the radio reports of more hazardous, wet, shin-deep snow on the roads and was about to groan after the announcer read the usual storm warning for snow—heavy at times, changing to rain—when she unexpectedly ended not with a complaint but with gratitude. "It's a real winter wonderland out there," she said genuinely. She reminded me and everyone else listening how comforting and typical this by-the-fire and cookie-baking weather was. She said the storm made the twinkling Christmas trees in all the wet windows appear especially bright in the gray dusk of midday.

I had invited four granddaughters (ages three to six) for a Christmas tea party with silver dollar pancakes, raspberries, and whipped cream served on my mother's good china, which I had inherited. Before they arrived, I turned off KHNS and put in a CD of Handel's *Messiah*. I even wore my mother's pearls to share our family tradition with them, so when they are old, they will hear this music and it will mean Christmastime. "And the government shall be upon his shoulders," the choir sang. I hoped there was something divine about governing.

Napkins were on laps, cookies on plates. The children asked to say grace and we held hands. I taught them how to pour the teapot and to sip, not slurp. Pinkies out. (Just for fun.) We said "please" and "thank you" and chewed with our mouths closed. We opened some presents their aunts in Juneau had sent—all books. Silvia Rose, the youngest at three, was totally impressed because the oldest, Caroline, could read "just like a grown-up." The Hallelujah chorus ended and the CD player switched to "Jingle Bell Rock," at which point they jumped up and danced, and the rainy wind blew, and the lights on the tree reflected in the windows as we poured the last of the peppermint tea into those delicate cups and saucers and nothing spilled and nothing broke.

True, I thought I might have seen some blood on Ivy's hand and Lani's leg, but that may have been juice from a raspberry (the ones I froze last summer are sloppy now), and, yes, there was a loud crash upstairs in the playroom (I was washing dishes in the kitchen by then) that is still unexplained. Silvia Rose cried, but only for about five minutes before falling asleep on the dog's bed. It was late in the short day and dark by then. Ivy took off all of her clothes at about the same time, maybe prompted by one of the new books her sister was reading, in which a polar bear loses his underwear.

But mostly the little girls' party was so perfectly civilized, and old-fashioned, that I felt like Super Grandma. I thought about how I'd handled things with Brad, and I thought maybe I would start to feel this capable, this calm and sure of myself, in assembly meetings. I considered imagining everyone in the next one wearing nothing but skivvies, like Ivy's polar bear. Maybe what Stephanie means when she says "living room" has more to do with confidence and competence than lighting and comfortable furniture. I was heading in the right direction. I just knew it.

BEFORE I GET back to the interim manager story, I want to give you some context from another meeting when my intuition, which I was sure was so very sound, led to trouble over something as benign as the appointments of volunteers to a couple of borough committees. This is all connected, because it was yet another time that keeping quiet would have been the judicious thing to do. But that's not what I did. The borough has many boards, committees, and commissions that advise the assembly and staff on everything from tourism and policing to the library and museum. The mayor has the authority to make the appointments, however the catch is that the assembly must approve them. It's a local version of the

constitutional checks and balances. These appointments are usually made on what is called the consent agenda—the items on this
agenda are approved automatically, by consensus, without debate,
because most of them are not a big deal. But at this particular
meeting there were two names that were controversial; at least I
thought so. One was a friend of mine, and the other a sort of foe.

Pizza Joe and Diana had not been respectful to assembly members and the staff, or others during the course of the harbor debate.
Diana was for the harbor; Joe was against it. Both were passionate about sharing their opinions. Which is fine. But the *way* they
argued for their positions was not. They were often belligerent and
confrontational. Due to *Robert's Rules of Order*, simply removing
two names from the mayor's list of appointees took a painfully cir-
cuitous path. It was almost as awkward as evaluating the manager
in public. First I had to pull all the committee appointees from
the consent agenda at the beginning of the meeting in order to
even discuss this, since they were listed together in one big batch.
Removing something from the consent agenda does not require a
vote, but it raises eyebrows. The mayor was not pleased, and I could
practically hear the "What's up?" look on Margaret's face when I
made my request, though she was Assemblywoman Friedenauer
again, all professional, by the time we got to it.

I had written down what I planned to say in order to make
sure I would be objective, considerate, and brief. My neck flushed
and my hands quivered as I gave my reason why Diana should
not be appointed to the harbor committee as non-personally as I
could. I knew I was hitting a hornet's nest with a stick but at that
time and place I felt it was worth it. I felt I needed to act locally
so politics in Haines, which was already on the edge of nastiness,

didn't sink further into a Trumpian sort of abusive anything-goes shout fest pit.

I did not repeat the ways Diana had berated assembly members or remind anyone that she called one member—Tom—both "stupid" and "despicable," or used an anatomically impossible term to denounce one of my own comments during a public meeting. I may swear when I speak to Beth about borough issues, or people that anger me, but that's private. Joe was supposed to be appointed to the Chilkat Center for the Arts advisory board. I objected to his appointment, too, because in plenty of very public meetings he had insulted former and current assembly members, the mayor, many of the fishermen, and Big Don and Diana. Even though I often agreed with Joe's opinions—after all, I am not in favor of the harbor project as proposed, either—and the rusty hunk of sheet metal strapped to his pickup as a permanent mobile protest of the steel wall was clever, his tirades sometimes made me wince. I did not need to detail any of this to the assembly. Everyone already knew the way Diana and Joe behaved. The mayor had chosen them for these committees anyway.

Instead, I noted that they both had spoken in ways that caused them to be perceived as harmful and disrespectful by residents, and because of that, they shouldn't hold positions of authority, because, I said, incivility only begets more incivility. I know. I cringe now sharing this. I must have sounded like a Quaker schoolmarm. Can I tell you how hard saving the world is, even one teeny tiny corner of it, when you are brand new at it? And how it is harder still to explain why this was so important to me? But I knew in my soul that it was. The Quakers taught me that which is morally wrong can't be politically right. Call me naïve, but I still believe that every small choice I make as a Haines leader adds to the millions of decisions, laws, and resolutions that collectively determine the way the United States of America is governed and carries us closer to the goal of "liberty and justice for all." This is the butterfly effect of democracy. The people I select to serve on advisory committees don't have to be Quakers, or even share my values, but they shouldn't curse me, or anyone else—even the people with whom I disagree, like Diana.

Assemblyman Jackson moved to "divide the question," in order to consider Diana and Joe's appointments separately.

Joe was confirmed and Diana wasn't.

Giving Joe a pass on his behavior but not Diana felt worse than if we had approved both of them. It was the opposite of what I had hoped to achieve: Fairness. One standard for everyone. Sure, I love Joe, but he had behaved badly. The other assembly members argued, though, that having Joe on the Chilkat Center board had nothing to do with his past harbor issues—"It's an arts center, for goodness sake," someone, I think Mike, had said—adding that we should be grateful for any citizen who volunteers. Joe is a performer, poet, and "feltist" (he makes artwork with scraps of felt). He could contribute positively there, they argued. His views on the harbor had nothing to do with the theater and shouldn't be a factor in the appointment.

Well, okay.

A place for everyone and everyone in his or her place is a good thing, but then why not approve Diana, even if I objected?

Turns out there was another reason. The majority of the assembly members felt that Diana should not be appointed because she was working against the best interests of Haines by fundraising for our former manager's legal expenses so he could sue us for firing him. It's not as if it was a secret. She was soliciting funds on Facebook. The police chief's wife had contributed $1,000. So Joe was placed on the Chilkat Center board, and Diana was left off the harbor committee. She would keep trying, though, and a year and a half later, would finally be appointed.

IF THIS WERE a melodrama on the Chilkat Center stage, organ music would play and the narrator would say in a hushed English accent, "And now the plot thickens, as our heroine returns to the assembly chambers for the surprising conclusion to our interim manager predicament."

I knew it would not end the way I had envisioned before the next meeting even began. I bumped into Brad in the entryway to the chambers, and eagerly asked him how his talk with the Juneau manager went. He said that he hadn't had time to give him a call and walked right by me. I had been so focused on my own plan, that I had been completely insensitive to Brad's feelings. He had said he wanted to be the permanent borough manager, and no doubt agreed to serve as the interim assuming that the longer, more public hiring process would favor the person already doing the job. The assembly's vote to choose an interim manager was tied. The mayor broke it in Brad's favor. I felt it was a lost opportunity, but the politics of it all meant that the cards were stacked against what I believed was best for the borough. The mayor framed it as the local favorite versus the out-of-town expert and worse, the same three assembly members—Tresham, Tom, and me—who objected to the harbor project, which Brad was managing, were now seen as trying to stop him from being interim manager. Brad had only limited managerial experience, but the rest of the assembly, and the mayor, wanted him, the real local, to be in charge. The line in the Code about hiring the most qualified candidate was interpreted to mean the one we knew the best, not the one with the stronger resume. And that is certainly one way to look at it. So, too, is the notion that Joe and Diana could serve the borough well in some ways even if they struggled in other ways. I have a higher standard is all. I wanted the best-qualified manager, and model citizens advising us. In my enthusiasm to do great work and solve a problem, I had miscalculated badly. I don't regret my choices those nights, but I would go about making them differently next time.

I HAVE NOT given up on Stephanie's advice about viewing the chambers as my living room yet, either. At Tresham's family's annual holiday open house, in a very large Officers Row home with enough room for lots of people who were full of cheer, I bumped into that crappy crabber. I should not think of him that way; let's change that to I bumped into a fisherman who is not a friend and disagrees with me about everything, especially the harbor project. We did not speak of crabs and sewer pipes, the manager woes, or politics at all. We talked instead about how wonderful being a grandparent is and the timely snowfall. It would be a white Christmas. The rain had finally quit, and flurries were falling gently on the now-white rooftops and lawns, and the boats in the harbor. The whole town looked like the inside of a snow globe, and there, by the fire in that lovely grand old parlor that has weathered more than its share of battles in the last hundred years, we pretended for a moment to be civil, and by doing so, we were.

Silence can be more productive than the cleverest of arguments. If I had not spoken to Brad, the outcome still would have been the same, but the consequences would not have. Likewise, the manager could have been let go without a public shaming. I didn't need to make that speech about civility, either, to promote it. In the future, I will try to choose my words more carefully, and wait at least a day before acting on my next brilliant idea. Just in case I have the urge to preach and teach again, I wrote, "Wait. Be Quiet. Think." on a sticky note and tacked it to my meeting calendar on my desk, put a log in the stove, unplugged the Christmas tree lights, and went upstairs to bed. "This is so hard," I said to Chip, who was reading. He did not say, "I told you so." He said, "I love you," and kissed me goodnight.

Manager and Committee Reports

Public Works repaired a broken water pipe and replaced an adjacent wall in a Chilkat Center bathroom and provided additional plowing and sanding to ensure the safety of residents attending the Woman's Club Holiday Bazaar at the school and the Lighting of the Library event.

Winter conditions continue, but thanks to the Chilkoot Indian Association we have a small sand truck on loan until the Public Works Department's primary sand truck is repaired.

The Harbormaster and Assistant Harbormaster have been keeping close watch on vessels in these heavy winds and have assisted with two that broke free.

Final edits of the 2017 tourism planner are underway.

SIX

Change of Address

CHIP WAS AWAY visiting his mother in Florida. I was home alone with the dogs—my own, plus the two I was watching for friends and family who were also away in warm places. I was living in a George Booth cartoon with fur flying everywhere. My plan was to spend the days writing, walking the dogs, stoking the woodstove, sipping tea, and eating vegetables. In other words, to give myself a week-long, stay-at-home retreat. I look forward to the few times a year when Chip is gone and I can recharge. I couldn't wait to watch the *Great British Baking Show* in bed on the iPad. I never do that when he's home.

My first day by myself turned into two meetings that lasted four hours each. I raced home in between them to let the dogs out, scarf down a peanut butter sandwich while standing up, and burn my mouth on hot tea trying to drink it quickly so that I would have time to check in on my neighbor Betty on my way to the next meeting. The planning workshop was about remodeling the kitchen at the Chilkat Center for the Arts. I suggested that the counter for the concession stand be moved as it has created bottlenecks during intermissions at performances for thirty years. Lee, a planning commissioner who lives next door to the Center and used to manage it and so knows the building intimately, thought we should dismantle an old staircase to the basement to create more space in the kitchen. He said there was another way to access the basement under the building. No one currently working for the borough knew about it, but Lee said the old cellarway had existed long before the second renovation, or maybe it was the third.

The Chilkat Center for the Arts began life as a cannery building across the Chilkat River from my house. It was floated over by the army about a hundred years ago and dragged up the hill by mules to its present location in historic Fort Seward, where it became a military entertainment and recreation hall. It has since evolved into the community performing arts center, which also hosts KHNS, yoga and martial arts classes, meetings, and my church on Sunday mornings, among other activities.

I was not required to attend the kitchen discussion, but as a member of the assembly I had been invited. Since the assembly would be the group doing the ultimate approving, and because I care about the future of the structure, and more importantly, the arts and recreation programs it houses, I went. The second meeting, though, was a command performance. I had to be there. It was a joint assembly, planning commission, and harbor committee meeting to choose a plan of action for repairing or replacing the town's freight dock. Groceries, lumber, fuel, and sometimes new cars all arrive in Haines on weekly barges from Seattle, and the old dock was falling apart and unsafe.

So instead of singing "Friends forget the cares that bore us, come and join the jolly chorus" at choir practice, I sat with a group of mostly men around a big horseshoe of folding tables in the lobby of the Chilkat Center, where the earlier meeting had also been held, and watched an engineer present a PowerPoint about our options for the dock. Lee and I, and Big Don, too, since he is on the harbor committee, all agreed on the same plan. Wonder of wonders, miracle of miracles—I felt like singing the tune from *Fiddler on the Roof.* How long ago did we all sing "Tradition" along with Tevye? What is the oldest Haines tradition? Arguing?

I willed myself to listen to Big Don and forget the recent past, especially the continuing threats of a recall. I figured since he wouldn't change his game plan, I could adjust mine.

As I sat in this second meeting trying hard not to be biased against Big Don—since we even agreed on the preferred design for this particular dock—I thought back to a previous planning commission meeting, and about how hard making changes can be. Holly Smith, the borough's newly hired staff planner who advises and helps direct the volunteer commission, praised a computer program called Parcel Viewer the borough had recently purchased. It maps structures and property and lists who owns them, their assessed tax value, and most importantly, their addresses.

We don't actually use them, and few of us even know our own. Addresses, I mean.

Directions to a garage sale might go like this: it's the blue house, or at least it used to be blue, the one up on the hillside, above Young Road, next door to the place that young couple bought from the old fisherman that the guy who worked at the post office remodeled after the basketball coach who was renting it moved out— didn't he win State with the Glacier Bears girls in 1985? That chat will lead to who was on the team, how many children the young couple have, and did the old fisherman die after that heart attack, or is he still living in Sitka? And that's the short version. Pretty soon you could be talking about the time the new teacher was boiling crab on the stove in the house across the road from where the garage sale is when a bear reached in the window and she ran upstairs and called 911 for help but didn't even know the name of the street she was living on: "It's dirt. Overlooking the harbor. There are tall spruce trees in front." Could have been any number of places. Finally the dispatcher asked who she was renting from, and when the new teacher said the old tourism director's name, the dispatcher replied, "Why didn't you say so in the first place?" As to the bear, that story never did rise to local legend status so it must have run off without incident.

Another big reason why conventional street numbers have not mattered in Haines is that we do not have home mail delivery. Everyone collects mail at the post office. Even little children know the family post office box number. PO Box 936 is my mailing address. It has been since I was twenty-four. I live at about Mile 2 on Mud Bay Road, across from the doctor's old house on the beach side.

Of course, that doctor doesn't even live in Alaska anymore.

Holly was determined to help all of us homeowners and tenants—and the emergency responders, visitors, police, Public Works department, and power company as well as the tax assessor—use proper house numbers, and this meant creating them, adjusting them, or relearning them. Some buildings had been numbered during brief bursts of historic organization and have addresses, but some of those no longer make sense because over time homes numbered, say, 100 and 101 back when they were the only two on a block now have three buildings in between them.

"Have any of you heard that show on the radio, the one with a guy named Al something? It's about safety, I think?" Holly asked and then continued, "Well, he was saying that people need to know their house numbers and that can be difficult because they are not always available." Holly paused for emphasis. "Not always available? This is not acceptable. Parcel Viewer will fix that."

To me, the noteworthy change here is that Holly didn't know who Fireman Al was. And why should she? He recently retired after decades as our town's much beloved paid fireman, though he still volunteers as a firefighter and also as an EMT on the ambulance crew. I thought everyone knew Al. Just like everyone knew that Lee knows all about the Chilkat Center and a lot of other things, for that matter. (For example, Lee can run the light and sound systems in the theater, operate the projector for the engineer's PowerPoint, and in a pinch host a music show at the radio station upstairs. He prefers blues and reggae.)

Al knew just about everyone and where they lived and when he didn't, he knew Haines well enough to figure it out fast. So did a lot of people. Giving directions based on landmarks or local names has always been the norm, but lately, when I tell the new reporter at the paper or a friend of my daughter's coming for a party that my house is about a mile from the top of Cemetery Hill, unlike Al, they don't know that the big hill has a name. And there is no signage to help them confirm which of the hills behind the Fort area I'm talking about. One more complication: there is no cemetery on Cemetery Hill. There used to be one, but the military graves were moved to the National Cemetery in Sitka after Fort Seward was decommissioned and Lee's parents helped purchase it after WWII.

No wonder that when Lee starts talking about history he can go on, and on, and on. During a meeting I once timed one of his lesser digressions on the problem with surveys at seventeen minutes. I found it fascinating and funny, especially the way he gesticulated with his hands, laughed, shook his head, and scratched his white beard. I remember when Lee's long hair was brown. At that particular meeting, his story did have a little bit to do with the decision at hand—whether to allow a garage to be built closer to the road right-of-way than Borough Code allowed—but really it was about why the paved road itself was not in the actual platted road right-of-way and why that meant that we really had no idea if the garage would be legal or not. Lee explained how this snafu, and others, were due to errors by a surveyor, long dead now, who happened to make a lot of mistakes. He was perhaps dyslexic, but since he was the only surveyor available in town for many years, he was hired by plenty of people and also by state and local agencies. Which is why today some lot lines and rights-of-way are off the mark. This system of looser boundaries worked fine until a property was sold or subdivided and then true surveys were required and suddenly half of one person's garden was in another's yard, and adjustments needed to be made.

It's no surprise that Garbage Point has been edited out of the lexicon of local place names, especially now that it's a favorite tour guide destination. Picture Point looks and sounds much better than the old dumpsite did, and I bet it has a real address on Parcel Viewer as well. The junk cars have been moved out, there's a new lawn and picnic tables, and a great view of town for visiting photographers. I noticed that no one advocated for a return to calling it Nukdik Point, the original name the Native people used for thousands of years. Nukdik means "young grouse." With all the activity there I have not spied any grouse, young or old. Downtown Haines was once known as Deishu or "end of the trail," by the only people who lived here at that time, and who spoke a language other than English. When I was first elected to the assembly, I suggested that we consider returning to the original name as it means more than plain old Haines, but nothing came of it. Mrs. Haines helped fund the Presbyterian Mission in 1881, which became the modern town and her name stuck, although she never lived here, or even visited. She was from Brooklyn.

PEOPLE HAVE BEEN living on this land a long, long time. Much longer than Fort Seward, which is on the national registry of historic places, but wasn't built until the first few years of the twentieth century. The original residents were the Tlingit people and they always knew where they were without any street signs or addresses, by the angle of the sun, the flow of the tides, the slope of the land, height of the trees, the ripeness of the berries, the thickness of ice on the river, wildlife migration patterns, or geographic landmarks like Nukdik Point. They named favorite places for what was obvious to anyone who called the area home: Little Spring, Fish Jumping Grounds, Where Everything from Afar Drifts Ashore, and Winter Village. The one remaining Native village in the region is Klukwan, "the Eternal Village," about twenty miles upriver from my house, and that site has been inhabited continuously for at least two thousand years. One of the three rivers that converge there is called the Klehini, which some people say means "mother's waters," as in amniotic fluid. Legend has it that the pregnant mothers of the first local babies waded across the river as their water broke and delivered them safely at what would become the village site.

THE FIRST NON-NATIVE explorers arrived here in the 1700s and met the powerful tribe of Chilkat Tlingits dispersed throughout many coastal villages and seasonal camps. Everything the Chilkats required came from the land and sea, but they were also skilled traders, and guarded the Chilkat mountain pass above Klukwan, controlling access to the tidewater from the interior of Alaska and the Yukon. The trading business, combined with plenty to eat—salmon, seals, game, and berries—gave the people of the Chilkat River valley a level of comfort, health, and wealth that allowed them time to carve and paint elaborate details onto everyday objects, such as house posts and storage boxes, to create ceremonial regalia, and to sing and dance. They carved wood and metal; beaded and sewed leather clothes and pouches; painted totem poles and canoes and paddles in rich red, black, and green pigments; and wove the iconic white, black, yellow, and light blue-green Chilkat blankets and dance robes out of mountain goat wool and cedar bark. They still do all of this, but it hasn't always been easy to maintain traditions. Lani Hotch lives in Klukwan and is recognized around the world for her exceptional weavings. She says that when she wears the old robes to dance in or for ceremonies, she feels the hands that created them, and hears the stories and the songs of her ancestors who were almost silenced along with her entire culture and way of life.

After the Christian missionaries arrived the Tlingits were forbidden to speak their language or practice any of their cultural arts. Little children, as young as five and six, were removed from their parents' homes and placed in boarding schools and made to wear stiff shoes instead of moccasins and eat oatmeal rather than fish and berries for breakfast, and worse by far, taught that everything their parents, grandparents, neighbors, and friends valued was wrong or downright evil. Can you even imagine those homes, those yards, those mealtimes, those celebrations, suddenly void of children, and the anguished silence where there once had been laughter and song? How could we be so cruel to one another?

WHEN JUNEAU AUTHOR Ernestine Hayes got stuck at our house because of an unexpected snowstorm, we stayed close to the hearth and kept our eyes on the weather in the unlikely event that a sudden break in the snow would last long enough for her to fly safely home in a small commuter plane, the only type that Haines's small airport can accommodate. State cuts to the winter ferry schedule meant there would not be a ferry in town until Monday, so that option was out, too. An Alaska Native, Ernestine was in Haines to read from her memoir, *Blonde Indian*, the title a reference to the fact that she was fair as a child and some people called her that. The change in plans was frustrating for Ernestine but it ended up giving us time for the kind of dicey, important conversations we would not normally have had, about race, privilege, history, education, the difference between growing up Native and poor as she had and white and well-off as I had, to name a few of the subjects we touched on.

At the time, Haines and Juneau were planning celebrations of the sesquicentennial anniversary of the Alaska Purchase by highlighting our connections to former Secretary of State William H. Seward. Ernestine asked, "Does anyone really believe Russia owned Alaskans and that they could 'transfer' us and it to the

United States?" She said it always irked her that Klondike stampeders were required to carry a thousand pounds of survival gear and supplies, enough to live for a year in the wilds of the north country or they'd surely perish. The Yukon and Alaska was not the moon. There were people living there, and they had food, they had shelter, they had families, Ernestine said. This territory was their home. All that changed when gold was discovered, and Alaska has never been the same since.

The non-Native townsite that began with Mrs. Haines's mission to convert the Tlingit people filled rapidly with outsiders after gold was discovered in the Porcupine Mining District. Then came the salmon canneries and the army and all the people who make modern Haines Haines: the dreamers and the builders, the lost souls and the entrepreneurs, the teachers and merchants, the preachers and pilgrims. Native and newcomer.

While I pondered the most appropriate way for Haines to acknowledge the Alaska Purchase, I made more tea and put another log in the stove. Ernestine told me of the time she had spoken to a group of volunteers at a women's shelter about her perspective as a Native woman who had suffered abuse, and had ended up trying very hard not to argue with a white social worker who insisted that she never notices color or race, and that everyone looks the same to her, which Ernestine thought was "absurd." I shared with her how my one brown-skinned daughter (Stoli was adopted) had recently been told by a friend of hers that she was "white inside," and that it was meant as a compliment. What was that person thinking? Ernestine nodded.

In *Blonde Indian* Ernestine writes about growing up in the old Juneau Indian Village—which is long gone, replaced by downtown development—in a bare wood-framed house without plumbing or insulation. Her grandmother cared for her because her mother was hospitalized with TB. Social workers who felt the conditions were below their standards intervened, and the state sent Ernestine to a Presbyterian orphanage and Native children's home in Haines. That building is also no longer standing, and much of the memories of it have not been shared in our collective community history. There are people in Haines who don't know it even existed and yet Ernestine lived there. Sometimes Haines House, as it was called, is mentioned in the obituary of a Native elder, but only briefly.

Ernestine managed to run away from the orphanage all the way to Idaho, winding up in California. Over the next twenty-five years or so she became so lost that she decided to return to the place where she began and start over. "I was finally homeless; I was finally broke. I was finally forty. I would go home now, or die with my thoughts facing north," she wrote in her memoir. She made it back to Juneau, attended college at age fifty, and by seventy was an English professor at the University of Alaska Southeast. She would go on to become the Alaska State Writer Laureate, a title she now holds.

She told the audience at the Haines library that home is not an address or a lot line. "Who our land now belongs to, or if land can even be owned, is a question for politicians and philosophers. But we belong to the land," she said. There is not one Tlingit person "who will not say, 'This is our land, for we still belong to it.'"

Bill, who is tall and white with a dark shock of hair that falls onto his glasses, volunteers at the library, sings bass in the choir, and lost his wife, the joy of his life, to cancer not very long ago, stood up and asked Ernestine if the land loved him, too—he whose ancestors were from Scandinavia and North Dakota and who had

spent most of his adult life in New Mexico and yet who, when he
arrived in Haines, knew in his bones that these mountains and
inlets were his home. Is it possible, he asked her, softly, that the
very ground we are standing on loves all of us?

My favorite place in the whole world is my own backyard. I
know how Bill feels. I have read how Ernestine feels. I have heard
her story. I have felt her grief. I'm not of this land the same way
Ernestine is but, oh, I love it. I wondered what she would say. I was
afraid of her answer.

"Yes," Ernestine replied to Bill. "The land loves those who love
it back."

THE TLINGIT PEOPLE take the long view of history,
which I was learning to remember as I reeled from one contentious assembly meeting to the next during the early part of my
term. Old and new ways, tradition and progress, my heart inclines
to Ernestine's and Lani Hotch's worldview, of slower times and
community values, of the land as eternal, our settlement on it as
ephemeral, that no one owns anything, we borrow it, we share it,
we leave it for the next generation, and the next and the next. But if
I start speaking like that while we're trying to figure out the Parcel
Viewer program, I might as well be talking for a half hour about
a surveyor who didn't know his geometry. Besides, we need house
numbers, or the ambulance may not be able to find me if I need to
call one when I'm old and have fallen down.

Holly's house-numbering campaign was working better than
I would have guessed. When Betty slipped in her kitchen on the
third day of my winter retreat, I dialed 911 and told the dispatcher
that an elderly woman has fallen and, although she says she is

okay, she has bumped her forehead, and there is a cut, and her leg hurts. I didn't want to alarm Betty, and it was not exactly an Emergency with a capital E. The flashing lights and siren won't be necessary, I told dispatch, but I think that Betty should go to the clinic just in case. Betty listened and shook her head "no," meaning she didn't need an ambulance. It was snowing hard. I didn't think she could manage her porch steps right then, or that I could safely move her down them and into my small car.

Betty has been struggling to live alone in her old home. She was afraid that her niece, or I, or the doctor, would insist she leave it, for her own good, and that an ambulance call may be proof that it was time to move to Haines Assisted Living. I knew that, but she was bleeding, and what if there were a crack in a bone that we couldn't see? I reminded the dispatcher and Betty, and myself, that in his Safety Report, Fireman Al always recommends calling 911 if there is any doubt more care may be required. Better safe than sorry is his credo. The dispatcher agreed. She knew Fireman Al. She asked for Betty's address.

"Excuse me?" She didn't know who Betty Holgate was? Holgate Creek is right there, next to Betty's house, I started to say, and realized that it is marked about as well as Cemetery Hill.

That's when Betty announced her house number.

She knew it?

"It's on the sign in my yard," she shrugged, more with the times than I was. It might be good to have a secure ride to the clinic, she said. Would I come too? Follow them in my car and bring her home when this nonsense was over?

When the ambulance arrived, Jenn, who is the new Fireman Al, was calm and thorough, and right away assured us that we did the right thing by calling her, that I had not overreacted. The two volunteers with her were, like Jenn, so gentle and skilled, that I was so grateful the town had this service, and how they seemed for all the world not to have anything more to do than help Betty and me.

They thanked Betty for posting her house number. It made their task easier.

At the clinic, the little gash on Betty's eyebrow was super-glued rather than stitched because the visiting medical student from Colorado said it would be a less painful procedure, and then she let us go home in my car.

Our new neighbor has already put up numbers on his house. They are brass and big enough to see from the road. He had shoveled and salted Betty's steps before I arrived the next day to check on her. Chip was home by then and Ernestine was back in Juneau when I attended the annual Elizabeth Peratrovich Day community potluck, not because I had to, but because I wanted to. The Tlingit leader had convinced the Alaska Territorial Legislature to ban discrimination against Natives on that day in 1945. I listened to the guest speaker at the potluck with a new sense of purpose as well as responsibility now that I was an elected leader. He said that Peratrovich's example teaches all of us to be aware of wrongdoing when we see it, even if it is the law of the land, as segregated schools and cafes were in her time, and that it takes courage to advocate for change, and patience and endurance to see it through.

Elizabeth was a reluctant activist. She and her attorney husband were told they couldn't rent much less own a home in the Juneau neighborhoods she preferred to live in because Natives were not allowed there. She couldn't send her children to the better, whites-only school or watch a movie in the good seats in the theater, and she had to walk by signs on downtown shops prohibiting "dogs and Indians" from entering. So she went to work. It took her three years to convince Alaska's lawmakers to pass the anti-discrimination act. Elizabeth, in her famous (to Alaskans anyway) speech to the legislature, arrived dressed to the nines, completely prepared, and confident. She spoke truth to power. When one senator argued, presciently, that outlawing racism and bigotry won't end it, she replied, "Then should murder be legal? It still happens, does it not?"

WHEN I FINALLY did learn my address, I wrote 1021 Mud Bay Road in thick black marker on an old orange fishing buoy and hung it in a tree at the end of my driveway so anyone who needed to could find our house. When the lupine and beach roses bloom in the spring, it will look pretty out there with all those blue and pink flowers underneath it.

What did James Taylor sing? The secret of life is enjoying the passage of time? A big part of me wants everything to stay the same, but change is inevitable, and often necessary. Sometimes it's better than the old ways. I would still like Haines to be called Deishu, but that could take awhile. Yes, we need addresses on our houses, of course we do, but we need to do right by the people this land loved first, the people who have always known that home is a place we know by name.

|||||||||||||||||||||||||||||||||||||||||||||||||||||||||||||||||||||||||||||||||||||

Manager and Committee Reports

Thanks to the Public Works crew the sand truck is up and running. It does raise bigger concerns that the sand truck is old, and we don't have a backup.

The tourism department is partnering with the Southeast Alaska State Fair to launch the first, and hopefully annual, Winterfest. It will include the traveling Telluride Mountainfilm Festival, the Miles Klehini Ski Classic and BBQ, a fat tire bicycle race, and a potential extreme ski and snowshoe race, the Kat to Koot Alpine Adventure Race up and over Mount Ripinski.

The Solid Waste Working Group met and asked and answered questions on what a solid waste plan needs to address. They concluded that enforcement, how to separate solid waste streams like food waste and recyclables, incentives to reduce waste, and long-term plans are needed. One question not answered was "When is a landfill full?"

The Planning Dept. is addressing lack of adequate bathroom facilities at the airport and researching Code revisions to allow for a "tiny house" development in town.

|||||||||||||||||||||||||||||||||||||||||||||||||||||||||||||||||||||||||||||||||||||

SEVEN

Be Kind, Be Brave, Be Thankful

A T THE BEGINNING of each assembly meeting I take my seat and pull out a clean copy of the agenda from the folder on the table in front of me. The one that comes with my fifty- or sometimes hundred-and-fifty-page meeting packet the week before is covered with notes and highlights, pages are folded over and papers clipped to one another. In that packet is everything from engineer's drawings for water plant improvements and cost comparisons of dump trucks to lists of activities in the Chilkat Center and photos from a new tourism brochure. There are the financial report, the manager's report, and the museum report. On the agenda itself I scribble a question regarding an amendment to the heli-ski tour area map and my thoughts on if we should approve the loan to the Haines Senior Village. I am thankful that the clerk provides a pristine copy for easy reference during the meeting since my own is such a mess.

In addition to the paper pile, I have that borough-issued iPad with all the meeting information on it and more. It's easier for me to use the paper. Since I work at a computer all day, when I prepare for meetings I prefer to be off a screen. Also, I sometimes read my packet in the bathtub while drinking a beer.

At the top of my clean agenda I always write: "Be kind, be brave, be thankful," and the name of a friend's granddaughter who was born with a serious brain condition that limits her growth physically and mentally. That one is to remind me to treat everyone as if they, too, carry a personal sorrow that is invisible, because don't we all? As a result of those first tense meetings, I sometimes add more self-coaching comments: "Meet hostility with courtesy," "listen," "smile," "ask questions," "wait before you speak." Sometimes I write "trust." So much comes down to trust. Who is telling the truth? Are they genuinely concerned for all of us or out for themselves and their friends? How can I tell?

When I was sworn in I solemnly promised to "Support the Constitution of the United States, the Constitution of the State of Alaska, and the Charter of the Haines Borough, and to faithfully perform the duties of the Borough Assembly to the best of my ability." I meant it. Although I am still not as steeped in all the meanings and nuances of the constitutions of my country and state as I should be, and the Charter of the Haines Borough and the Haines Borough Code that goes with it are over five hundred pages long and contain contradictions that nobody notices until there is a problem, my decisions must be based on these rules. Certainly, judgment plays a role, too, as do so many other factors. Nothing occurs in a vacuum.

It's a lot of responsibility. No wonder that in the beginning I was so nervous that when I wrote my advice to myself on the agenda, I pressed hard on the pen to keep it from shaking. As the months go on, my tremors have become less frequent. It's kind of like being a mother—it's terrifying to think this little life is in your hands, but with each birth or adoption you are surer of your abilities to care for a child. But it's always hard to know anything for sure. I was already a grandmother when doctors decided it was unsafe for infants to sleep on their tummies, as I had been taught, and instead should rest on their backs. I really felt scared about doing this with my grandchildren, but my daughters insisted, and their physicians and all the baby books were emphatic about it, so I adapted.

My years of cycling and running marathons might provide a better metaphor. Once I realized that governing was not a sprint, as the lightning pace of news flashes and the urgency of campaigns and social media comments would have us believe, but rather an endurance event, I relaxed. There is no room for a stumble in a hundred-meter dash, but a marathon is forgiving. I even walked for a few terrible minutes in the race where I clocked my fastest time. Here's something I don't say out loud, but I will tell you now: sometimes, when I'm frustrated with a burly man in work boots and a pro-mining bumper sticker on his truck who says he's against funding the library, I imagine trouncing him in a bike race. Will I ever grow up?

Some people can create a conflict out of anything. During the public hearing on an otherwise popular proposal to ban plastic shopping bags that I had sponsored at the request of the sixth-grade class and Haines Friends of Recycling, one newer assembly member exploded. (There are annual elections for two of the six assembly seats; some members have remained and some have left during my three-year term.) The self-proclaimed progressive said that the ordinance did not go far enough and that all single-use plastic items in Haines should be banned or taxed so high that no one would use them, ever! Then another assembly member argued against the exemption for plastic bags that hold fish, meat, or bulk items like rice and candy. The ordinance was saved when we all took an imaginary trip to the store with our cloth bag, and pictured ourselves dropping in a piece of chicken, a bunch of grapes, and a scoop of rice, until everyone broke into fits of laughter and the original bag measure passed. And, yes, we all agreed that there was much more work to do to eliminate plastics from the environment but at least we had begun. Right here in Haines.

Rabbi Abraham Joshua Heschel once said that when he was young, he admired clever people, but after he grew old it was the kind people he looked to for leadership. The older I am, the more I realize that to be a kind leader—or just a kind person in a world that increasingly values caustic comments and contrarian quarrelers—requires courage. And sometimes inspiration comes from unlikely sources. Take Evelyna, a thoughtful elderly lady who attends many of our meetings. I say elderly, but I bet we are close to the same age. She is more solid, and has more gravitas, more wisdom, and seems much surer of herself than I am. She can walk up to the microphone following one of Big Don's complaints and completely disagree with him, in the nicest way. She can do the same with a contractor, tour operator, the assembly, and borough staff.

I don't know Evelyna's story—she is a private person—but when I see her walking home with her dog and her wagonload of groceries and library books, the same wagon she uses to pick up trash on the side of the road, I know that she represents the best of us. She walks to assembly meetings from the nearby mostly low-income Native neighborhood where she lives with her dog, Suki, whom she leaves tied by the door. She doesn't own a car.

During the Haines Harbor hearings Evelyna asked why the project was being designed only for owners of boats and trucks when the waterfront belonged to everyone. She said she would like to see a balance between the areas designated for launching and parking and those where she and Suki can stroll or sit and enjoy nature.

That didn't go so well. But Evelyna took it in stride.

I don't even remember what the issue was the day Evelyna reminded us that we are a community of caring people first, and that the role of politics in our lives is probably not even a close second. On that night, Evelyna asked the mayor if she could trade her three minutes of public comment time for three minutes of silence, with the hope that we may think better of one another and to remind ourselves why we love this place. Much to my astonishment, the mayor agreed. Desperate times call for desperate measures and all that. We sat in the unusual, almost comfortable quiet, bolstered by Evelyna's sincerity, as the clock on the wall ticked. I know, it's not a big deal in the grand scheme of things, but how can we even begin to tackle the pressing issues of our time, from climate change and social justice to income inequality and access to healthcare—not to mention all those plastic bags in the trees at the dump—if we won't speak or listen to one another? Conflict may feed great headlines, but a steady diet of it is killing us.

The Charter, which I have sworn to uphold, declares that a primary purpose of our government is to be responsive to its citizens. To that end, the Code has an ethics clause, which guides us when relationships with one another or with businesses may hinder treating everyone equally, from Evelyna to Big Don.

There are layers of personal and political associations, and some reach back generations, but there are two legal types of conflict of interest for elected officials that I have been instructed by the borough attorney to declare, if they arise. I am also obliged to ask other members of the assembly to do so, too, if I believe their judgment may be compromised. The first is defined by a substantial financial interest. It is assumed that money has the greatest power over people, and that no one will be fair when their bank account balance is at stake, so anyone with that issue must be removed from the discussion and the vote. Money is the original sin of politics, I guess. The second type of conflict is legally known as bias and it concerns how our closest relationships may influence our decisions. Obviously an assembly member may not discuss or take action on issues involving immediate family members (spouse and children) but friendships, or for that matter, grudges, don't count and they are a factor in every single meeting in a small town.

The part-time borough attorney, who lives in Anchorage and speaks to us on the phone, said that member recusal is discouraged because when any one of us is removed from decision-making and debate it results in one less representative of the people, and that is not fair to voters. If we prohibited one another from voting due to bias, the entire assembly, as well as the mayor and manager, would never be able to make a decision on anything. I often wish I could get out of casting votes that may anger or please close friends and relatives, but this kind of conflict does not meet the letter of the law.

For example, my younger sister Suzanne lives in Haines and everyone knows who she is and that she and her husband are appealing the cost of a water line extension to their property. If I support lowering the price for the line it could appear to be favoritism, even if that is the right thing to do. I know it will cause tension at Thanksgiving dinner if I don't, even though that may be the right choice, and of course family harmony is not a valid reason for adjusting the price of a water line extension. I recused myself from the first discussion but was later informed that I shouldn't have by the attorney. There would surely be more.

Still, what's in the best interest of most of the residents is sometimes hard to know, and the Haines Borough Charter and Code don't always have the answer. It's critical to try to answer that question, though, because just as Tom noted that the former manager's salary was coming from the people's "dough," so, too, are the salaries and equipment of the Public Works department crew who will dig the pipe and hook up the line. The rate charged to my sister affects whether there is money to repair the sidewalk that Evelyna uses to pull her wagon on. Everything we do, every decision we make, is connected to the greater good (or harm) of the community and "the community" is not a list of numbers in the phone book. It's faces, names, families, friends, and enemies, who live together, for better or worse, 'til death (or a one-way ticket out of town) do we part.

No wonder I can't sleep nights after meetings.

Thank goodness for that "best of my ability" clause in the oath of office, because sometimes creating a matrix of benefits and costs doesn't allow me to vote for what I believe is most moral. An example: Using public funds to help residents of a housing complex for the elderly by spending thirty thousand dollars to pay for a consultant to create a business plan may not be everyone's idea of a wise use of borough dollars since it only directly benefits about fifteen people. But to the "best of my ability," I thought it was. Sometimes you just have to do the right thing for a group of people you care about, even if it may cause some harm to borough finances as a whole and set what the manager and chief financial officer call "a precedent." By which I'm pretty sure they mean a problem for future assemblies.

The Haines Senior Village, a block of modest, single-story, one- and two-bedroom apartments across the street from the Senior Center and an easy walk to the library, park, and Mountain Market, is a nonprofit organization. They discovered they were in financial trouble due to a large balloon payment on their mortgage that somehow their board and manager were not aware of. This happens. The mortgage papers had been signed decades before. People come and go, literally (the residents who started the Senior Village have died), and memories fade. The seniors had a senior moment. They asked the borough to loan them close to $200,000 so they could pay their bill, and to consider an even larger refinance package on the entire mortgage.

My friend Joan, who swims with me at the pool, is a resident there and so is an elderly couple from my church. Would I be biased? When the relatively young fellow resident Chuck Mitman ushered those mostly women elders, with their walkers and canes, into the assembly chambers on a wet, dark night, I smiled and thanked them for coming as he helped them to their seats. To me, the retired nurse, teacher, librarian, shopkeeper, and choir director are like the grandparents of our town. Chuck's presence spoke volumes as well. A Vietnam veteran and member of the American Legion, Chuck also has stage IV cancer and seems determined to do as much good and be as kind to as many people and animals as he can before his time is up. He volunteers on the board of the animal rescue kennel and the ambulance squad. He cares about people, especially the aged and infirm, or those who may be down on their luck. He has dramatic tattoos, and a limp from a logging accident, and rides an immaculate red Harley with a sidecar for his dog, Doc. I trust Chuck.

My seat was so close to the microphone where public testimony is given that I could practically read the notes in the manager of the Senior Village's quaking hands. It's okay, I whispered, and wished I could tell her that I know it's hard to stand up and speak in here, that doing so makes me shake sometimes, too.

We spent several more months debating whether to loan the money to the seniors. Finally we came up with another solution. We agreed to hire a consultant for $30,000 to work with their lender and guide the Senior Village on a sustainable course of action that may not require spending significant public funds. The key here is "may not"—in fact, we could still have to pay the bill if this fails. It's worth the risk. I loved voting to help them, and I justified it by my bias. Also, if the borough could spend $30,000 on a study to confirm helicopters are noisy after we turned down a heli-ski tour operator's request to build a heliport in a rural neighborhood closer to the mountains than the airport, surely we could use the same amount to help our elders. You can't put a price on the value of keeping the Senior Village healthy, because, with any luck, one day we will all be old and need a secure place to live, too.

To say I was not as sympathetic to the critical young engineer who always introduces himself with the name of the company he works for and then chastises us in a tone suggesting that we have the IQs of earthworms as I was to the seniors is an understatement. When he took the microphone to suggest improvements to a waterfront trail design, I conducted a personal bias assessment and decided I was predisposed to disagree with anything he said. The feeling was apparently mutual, and everyone knew it, but I still owed him, and all speakers, my attention. So I listened. It was the least I could do.

I have sat in that same seat and felt waves of emotion wash over me during many public hearings. Sometimes it's anger, sometimes it's fear that I will do the wrong thing, and sometimes it's joy—we got rid of plastic bags!—and sometimes it's respect. Respect for Evelyna, for the senior citizens, and for the process, as preachy as that sounds. The hardest and the easiest part is knowing mostly everyone who speaks at the microphone. When residents testified for an hour on what the assembly's position should be in a letter we were planning to send to the state agency considering granting a permit for a wastewater treatment plan at a mine exploration site, I knew a lot of them and was impressed. Many others in the room nodded in silent agreement.

The permit offered a potentially precedent-setting plan for wastewater treatment at what may one day be a large mine. I was inclined toward the residents who favored caution and who sought more information and more time to digest the company's two thousand–page permit application. Just about everybody present, including the president of the nonprofit watershed council, which is nonpolitical, said that the plan was threatening to the nearby rivers and salmon, and they pleaded with the assembly to request that it be rewritten and resubmitted. At the very least, they said, we should ask the state for a ninety-day extension on the comment period to allow concerned citizens time to better understand what was going on at the remote exploration site.

Though the public comments in the room were mainly against approving the application, many other residents had sent emails in support of the mine plan moving forward, sported bumper stickers promoting mining, and were not concerned with the river but instead favored the jobs the mine may create someday. One email noted that fishermen kill fish for a living, so why can't miners kill a few?

Tom and I tried to suggest a sixty-day comment period extension, but that failed, and we wound up with a thirty-day one. We succeeded in removing the language the manager and mayor had put in the letter declaring that the borough's intent was to work with the company to see the mine develop. That seemed a big leap from where most residents' hearts were. We also included a list of concerns about the wastewater, waste rock, avalanches, monitoring of the site for problems, and more.

What still bothers me, though, is that in the end, the representative of the Canadian company running the project—their "expert"—had more sway with the assembly and the borough staff than everyone else in the room. Why was that? Was it money again? There was at least one pro-mine supporter not affiliated with the company who spoke up. "Dakota Fred" is the star of a reality television show about gold mining filmed near the proposed project. "Any of you people businesspeople?" he bellowed dramatically at the assembly. As he boasted that his little placer mine will spend "$160,000 a week" this summer in Haines, he looked right at me. He knows I'm married to Chip. He is a good customer at our store. He was reminding us all about how the money the mine brings would be shared in the community, and to him that fact outweighed any damage done to the Klehini and

Chilkat River salmon. This is where the law and my conscience differ. I won't remove myself from this vote for potential conflict of interest. The money Fred or a new mine may spend in our lumberyard does not motivate me the way it does Fred. I know my family will make more money if a mine is built, but we could lose a different kind of wealth worth much more. No wonder some mine proponents think I'm crazy and incompetent.

After Dakota Fred—who lives in Louisiana, is named for a different state, and stars in a show about Alaska—marched out, the large clump of environmentalists looked puzzled. One woman asked loudly, "Who was that guy?" Since most of them did not watch television at all, they had never heard of Dakota Fred, or the hit show called *Gold Rush* that began in Haines and stars our own Parker Schnabel, Roger's son.

After one of my first assembly meetings, Big Don's son Donnie stopped me in the parking lot and asked if I had a minute. We had worked well on the planning commission together. He owns and operates the family construction company now that "the old man," as he calls his father, had retired. Donnie and I don't agree on a lot. He loves a clear-cut. I love a forest. But I kind of like him and I think he kind of likes me. He was very upset and told me that when he looked at the assembly that evening—I think we had talked about landscaping at the harbor, again-—he didn't see the Haines he lives in. There is no one, he said, who represented him. "I grew up in this town and I don't recognize it anymore, and that makes me sad. I want you to know that, is all." I said I was sorry, and I would remember what he said.

As we debated this new mining permit, I saw what Donnie meant when none of the people against it recognized Dakota Fred.

They live in different worlds. I don't want to think in those "Us" versus "Them" terms, but that does not mean that I should side with Donnie and his father, who support a mine permit that could pollute our river, just to show him that I see what he means, and that I care. I do want to consider his opinion. Should he weigh in on, say, my sister's water line extension discussion, which is still ongoing, I might even agree with him because he is an expert on that sort of thing. Also, the deliberations on the mine will continue. That preliminary permit was granted in spite of the comments against it, although I believe that voicing objections may still change the outcome, someday.

THE SUNDAY AFTER the Trump victory I spoke at a Unitarian church in Anchorage. The reading had been scheduled months ahead of time and was supposed to be about my most recent book. Instead, I ended up fielding questions about what the election meant and wishing we all could find some positive way to react. It wasn't easy. I told the devastated liberal audience that in Haines that morning, the Presbyterians for Hillary or Bernie or whoever were sitting next to Presbyterians for Trump. The pastor at the largest church in our town was not consoling his congregation—because some of his parishioners were celebrating. Ron Horn no doubt stuck to the Bible lessons. He usually does. He may have focused a little more on the words Jesus used when teaching his followers: to love God and love one another, or Micah 6:8, to act justly, love mercy, and walk humbly, but I don't know because I wasn't there. When I admitted to the Unitarians that at least two of my dear friends and many people I know and have hosted in my home voted for Trump, they gasped.

My friend Becky and her husband, Don (not to be confused with Donnie or Big Don), attend that Presbyterian church, and her faith is the kind that trusts God will catch her by the back of her red Swedish sweater before she crashes to the bottom of a cold, dark crevasse. I believe it's why she still climbs out of bed most mornings. That, and the fact that though she has lost three of her six children to accident, suicide, and cancer, "I have to love my three kids, and the grandkids who are still here. They need me. I need them. It's how I keep moving even when I don't want to, like this morning," she told me as we walked on the beach one day. Her pretty gray curls blew every which way.

"I think it's normal to stay in bed with the covers over your head, considering," I said.

On the last night of her son Aaron's life, Becky and Aaron played Scrabble and she won. Aaron told Becky he was walking home. They lived on the same downtown street. His body was found the next day in Don's backyard shop.

Becky and Don didn't want to be at their house right after that, and with all the company coming for the funeral they needed more room, so at our invitation they moved into ours for a short while. So did some of their children and grandchildren and a few more friends and family from near and far. Everyone in town, it seemed, marched in and out all day and night to love and comfort them. Stuff was everywhere. Boots and coats, boxes of food. The fridge was plugged, casseroles and cookies covered the counters, and more were wedged in the freezer. There were crying babies, wet dogs, burning bacon, and endless cups of coffee from a couple of additional coffeemakers crowding the counters. Chip and I slept in the loft above the garage. I welcomed people who had been at odds with me in meetings, and they washed the dishes in my sink.

One evening old friends arrived with two potpies baked from a neighbor's chicken, which Don's bird dog Stitches had killed a few days before, and then they began frying up moose steak, too. "It makes a greasy mess," Craig said, dropping hunks of battered meat in a pan that spit hot oil all over the stove and the rack of clean pots hanging above it. "But, man, is it good. Try some?" Later, we would support Craig during his own public grieving of a very different kind.

By the fire, near midnight when the house was finally quiet, Becky rocked a grandbaby named after one of her lost sons and I sat on the couch with Stitches while my golden retriever slept on the rug. We were all exhausted. I wondered if Becky and I would ever return to the luxury of fretting about life's small troubles, after sharing such a big one.

She looked at the dogs and said, "You may want to check Pearl."

"Why?"

"Stitches has lice."

THE HOUSE I grew up in on Long Island had lots of space for unexpected guests. Eight bedrooms. But we didn't have neighbors or even relatives who sought refuge with my parents when the worst thing that could happen to them did happen. What a great gift it is to have friends like Don and Becky. What good fortune I have had to spend my whole adult life in a place where neighbors have become the kind of people, as Robert Frost sort of said, who when they come to my door I welcome them.

At the grocery store the other day, Wayne, a former Kansas wheat farmer and friend of Becky's, asked if I had a minute to talk. Wayne had bought a boat and captained it from Seattle to Haines, to ease his grief after his daughter and son-in-law died while mountain climbing in Europe on their honeymoon.

"Sure," I said to Wayne.

"I have a question for you. Ready?"

"Yup."

"What makes a good life?"

The teenage checker looked at Wayne and back at me and laughed.

"I'm serious," Wayne said to him, and to me. "You must have insights from all the obituaries you write, but I will give you some time to think about it and call in a week or so."

"I can answer you now," I said. "Relationships. I believe that in the end what matters is love. That we loved and that we were loved."

"Yes! I knew it," Wayne said. "Thank you."

WHEN ALL WAS said and done, I did not have to decide about my sister's water line. She and her husband sold the lot and the new owner had no objection to the borough's fees. There were other meetings devoted to potentially controversial issues. In one, a newly elected assemblyman, a fisherman, wanted us to pass an ordinance banning the underwater storage of hazardous materials. Mine tailings, the rock and dirt left over after the valuable minerals are extracted, can be hazardous, and the lined pools designed to keep them from dispersing in nearby land, air, or water by covering them with water (called tailings ponds) are a common feature of mines. But this method of containment has historically failed, with disastrous consequences for everything living downstream.

The proposed ordinance would not target a mine specifically—that was not legal in Alaska. It would ban all underwater storage of hazardous materials. Since it did not mention mine waste, its proponents, and the new assemblyman, said it wasn't singling out one project or company. No one would be able to put, say, nuclear waste in a big pond, either, if it passed. The mining company and its supporters pushed back. The usual environmentally minded people pushed forward with predictable points that were duly noted. We were nearing an impasse.

Then someone cut from Evelyna's respectful, well-liked cloth spoke, except that he was not a regular presence at meetings. The high school basketball coach, who has won two state championships with the small but talented Glacier Bears boys' team, stood up. We all support the team, and the coach. He grew up in Haines, is not a political guy, rarely speaks in public, and has such a cool head that even during the biggest games he's calm. Now he took the microphone and was not happy. He said, look guys, it's a no-brainer that if you know your history at all, you know you have to keep your watershed clean. He said he supported anything that helps to do that, including this ordinance, thanked us, and then sat down.

It is not as if we all held hands and agreed to suddenly change. The coach didn't have any notes and he didn't speak for his allotted three minutes. He offered no additional geochemical data to persuade us. As far as I know, the coach was guided by his own conscience, though no doubt influenced by his son-in-law, who happened to be the new assembly member that had introduced the ordinance. But we all knew the coach would bench his own son if he needed to, and had before. His message was simple: protect the river. That led to opponents agreeing that the volume of water in the ordinance should be specific: were we talking paintbrushes in a jar? And hazardous waste needed to be defined: would this outlaw septic tanks? That was not the intent. The ordinance was sent to a committee to fine tune before, hopefully, its final passage. There was no hurry. The language and intent needed to be tight and clear. When a new and trusted voice enters an old conversation, a voice that hasn't spoken before, and states the obvious, attitudes shift. Having the same people line up on the same side of issues over and over, rarely, if ever, has changed anyone's mind.

WHEN I WRITE "meet hostility with courtesy" on my agenda and "listen," I am mindful of all these things, but when I write, "be kind, be brave, be thankful," I take a deep breath. This was Becky Nash's prayer for my only son. She is his godmother and wrote those words in a card she gave him before he left for a year in Australia. She wrote it again on the chalkboard in our mudroom after Aaron died. My job writing obituaries at the *Chilkat Valley News* helps keep politics in perspective. Some people, my favorite ones often, devote their lives to causes that they care about, that make the world a better place, from parks and preschools to mental healthcare and the arts. Their families proudly note those accomplishments and commitment to them, especially in the face of adversity. When I write obits, no one has ever asked me to tally Grandpa's wealth, or make sure readers know what presidential candidates he voted for. A graduation date, the names of their children, or the way the sun caught Aaron's smile when he soared through the air on his snowboard are all more relevant in the end than money and politics. Issues, maybe. Such as that they cared about family planning or were instrumental in developing the tourism industry. But politics, no.

When three old-timers passed away very close together, Tom was more down than I had ever seen him. Hertz, the electrician who organized the Fourth of July raft race, and Leo, the logger who volunteered for the fair, were the kind of people who didn't automatically choose sides. "Heath, I don't know if I want to live in a Haines without these guys, much less serve on the assembly," Tom said. The assembly meetings were beating us up. Every decision we made and everything we said was being challenged by the same people who wanted us to hire Brad permanently, were hoping to catch us violating the law or ethics standards, and who continued to drum up support for a recall on Facebook. Tom's wife is Australian. He could join my son on the beach over there and never return. I don't know whether the old-timers were Republicans or Democrats, whether they voted for Trump or Hillary. And it didn't matter.

Lawrence was the third elder to pass on, and he had always been so friendly, and took care to do nice work when he operated heavy equipment for road projects while making improvements to the sewer and water in his home village of Klukwan. He was a longtime volunteer and participant in a snow machine race that Diana was involved in as well. She was my best source for those details. I hesitated to call her, considering how she felt about me, and about the world, the mine, and energy-efficient cars. I pretended she never made that crack about the parking lot at the harbor being so big because it was meant for working men's trucks like hers and not little Subarus like mine. She has a pretty garden.

I could praise it. And I had delivered her husband's eulogy, before everyone had become diehards in red or blue uniforms.

When she picked up the phone, I said, "Hi, Diana, it's Heather." I heard her pause. I imagined her thinking, "What does *she* want?" That's my problem, isn't it? I smiled as I spoke. You can hear a smile. "I'm calling about Lawrence. I know you were his friend and I'd like to talk with you about him for the obituary." I thought I could hear her relief when she said she'd be happy to help and thanked me for calling her. She shared some of their snow-machining adventures and spoke of how much he loved watching his grandkids play basketball. Lawrence was such a nice man, we agreed. "We've lost so many good ones lately," Diana said, echoing Tom.

I GAVE AARON'S eulogy because, like Diana had, his parents asked me to. I began: "Aaron was an often-exuberant, standout artist, skateboarder, snowboarder, outdoorsman, and fisherman who suffered from bipolar disorder. It was what made him the remarkable person he was, and what shortened his life." His strength was his weakness, or was his weakness his strength? Isn't that true to some degree for all of us?

Afterward, I could not stay for the coffee and cake reception in the Chilkat Center lobby. I left Chip there with the excuse that I had to prepare for what I knew would be a kind of wake at our house for close friends and family. I had held up well while speaking, but I was sobbing by the time I hit Cemetery Hill, windshield wipers flapping. I let myself into our blessedly silent home and, sliding a crusty pan of lasagna aside in order to wash a glass, I tipped some wine into it from the half-empty box and took it in by the fire. I nudged Stitches off the couch, didn't see any bugs moving on her or it, gathered the children's books and magazines from the floor, patted Pearl, and leaned back onto an opened baby food pouch. Applesauce squirted onto my best sweater and the sofa cushions. "I want my life back," I cried.

The couch was crooked, so I pushed it back in place, and stubbed my toe on a Scrabble box. It was Becky's. "Oh, honestly!" I wailed. Aaron is never coming back to my house at Easter to eat the whole platter of asparagus vinaigrette, or to any house for any meals. He'll never play this game again, will he? My abundance of healthy children and grandchildren felt downright ostentatious. One of the books on the shelves by the fire is titled *The Matter Is Life* by J. California Cooper. What was the matter with me? Life, that's the matter. There's too much of it. I wept for Becky and Don, and for my son who surfed and worked with Aaron all those eventful summers on Don's fishing boat, and who was now so far away in Australia swimming with sharks, and for Diana, too, and how lonely she must be in her empty house on rainy nights without her husband, and for all of us, tumbling up and down in love and loss and community and family in what feels like an old washer that's overloaded and off-balance.

I LEARNED THAT Don and Becky were voting for Trump while watching the Cubs play on the big TV in my son-in-law's basement. Don squeezed my hand and said, "I voted for my favorite liberal today." He was leaving for a hunting trip up north and had filled out an early ballot in case he wasn't home on Election Day. He wanted me to know he had chosen me for the assembly. He decided to vote in the presidential election while he was at it. I know he is conservative, and mostly Republican, but when he said, "I picked Trump" and then, "so I guess you can cancel me out," I looked at his hand on top of mine, and the smile crinkles around his blue eyes, and wondered if, for just a heartbeat, this was my moment to take a stand against Trump and what he stood for, and just as quickly, decided it was not.

No one can get out of making decisions that may anger or please close friends and relatives. Just ask my children how happy they were with my rules when they were teenagers. Most of us don't have to make them as publicly as I do, but many choose to attack people who don't share their views on social media. It is unkind, and unnecessary. I had hurt people I cared about by voting against the harbor contract. Or, viewed the other way, they had taken my actions personally, but what difference did it make if it was intentional or not? The sting we all felt was real. Why harm relationships if you don't have to? Instead, be *for* something: suicide prevention, clean water, eldercare, childcare, libraries, bumblebees, the home team—and advocate for them with kindness, courage, and gratitude, knowing that your voice may just be the one that makes the change you hope for. That will never happen if the people you need to convince won't listen to you because you are no longer speaking to them.

Even though politicians should not talk in absolutes, and should be open to compromise, even at the smallest level of the government in which they serve, and be aware of bias and reject it when they sense it happening, I can say with certainty that I am never shunning Don and Becky over who they vote (or don't) vote for. I am not giving Trump or any politicians or parties or organizations left or right that power. That's not how my world turns.

Don and I have never mentioned the president again, not at Christmas or Easter, not when he's watching the Mariners games on TV with Chip or dropping off some fresh cod from his boat. Becky stopped me in the hall at school, though, a few months into the Trump administration, when we were both picking up grandchildren and said, "What was I thinking when I voted for that man?" I replied, "Don't blame me," and while I would like to say this was a big deal, it really didn't change a thing between the two of us.

Manager and Committee Reports

Chief Scott reports that the police department is significantly over budget due to overtime costs and emergency responses. The Public Safety Commission requests that the assembly amend the budget to fund the $63,000 shortfall.

The harbor crew did an excellent job of notifying boat owners during the weekend snowstorm and shoveling off vessels as necessary. However, despite their efforts, one vessel sank.

There has been a request for lighting on the sledding hill, but there are concerns that lights at night could bother nearby residents, so we are looking into an automatic timer to turn them off at a reasonable hour.

At the Chilkat Center for the Arts, the Chit Chat Cafe "River Talk" storytelling series winter season continues. Haines's own Geppetto's Junkyard puppet troupe brought "Travels in the Belly" to the stage for a command performance after touring Skagway and Petersburg, and the Haines Arts Council presented Women of the World in concert. Ongoing yoga, martial arts, fitness classes, and church services for St. Michael and All Angels continue.

Winterfest was a great success despite the storm-related road and ferry closures and the basketball games conflict.

EIGHT

Glorious Chaos

'M THINKING ABOUT the line on the last page of the form that the clerk asks residents to fill out when they want to appeal a decision of the planning commission or the assembly. Clerk Julie Cozzi poses this question: "The remedy is?" and leaves a space for their preferred resolution.

The outcome is rarely the one they wanted, though, because the assembly almost always either upholds the original decision or finds a way to compromise. A total reversal is rare. Ideally, we resolve it in a way that is acceptable to both parties but, in reality, no one is thrilled. "It could be worse" or "I can live with that" is the best we can hope for. In politics, as in religion, making any concession is difficult. Demanding that the other side compromise is easy, as long as your side doesn't have to. When you do, it can mean abandoning values, standards, morals, beliefs. Selling your soul to the devil. That is true, absolutely, on major moral issues, like civil rights, the environment, or healthcare; I get that. Some things are sacred. There must be places where elected officials draw the line and say no, and "quite frankly," as my campaign manager Teresa prefaces the points she wants to underscore—if I hadn't then I never would have been elected. "I will always compromise" was no one's campaign slogan, ever. Neither was "I will change my mind." I learned something about both when our police chief requested adding a fifth officer to his department and more overtime pay in order to support twenty-four-hour patrols.

After doing a little research I discovered that the bars in Haines are only required to be closed for three hours a day. You are reading that correctly. Alaskan state law allows bars to serve alcohol seven days a week from 8:00 a.m. to 5:00 a.m.—that's twenty-one hours straight. This was adding pressure on the police department to have officers on duty and on standby in the wee hours. It made sense to me that there was a correlation between drinking and late-night disturbances. Towns may impose stricter laws than the state requires, and some do—for instance, waiting until noon on Sunday to open and closing at 2:00 a.m. on weeknights—but Haines hadn't done so. In a committee meeting I had floated the idea of curtailing bar hours, to save on police costs and keep the town safer at night.

Around this time, I was in the middle of writing an obituary for a woman who had lived in Haines from the 1960s to the early 1990s and was fairly prominent in town. Her sons were great high school basketball players, and she worked at the bank. But there were few people alive who remembered her well enough for me to interview about her life. Pioneer Bar owner Christy Tengs Fowler knows everyone. She grew up in the bar that was originally her father's and has a good memory. Christy is also a poet, songwriter, and my friend. So I called her up. She remembered Dorothy. She told me how smart and funny her former next-door neighbor was, and how Dorothy and Christy's mothers would share a cocktail in the afternoon while Christy played the piano for them.

Before we hung up Christy changed the subject. She had a gripe with the assembly. "I read in the paper someone wants to close the bars early. I'm totally against that. We have enough trouble now competing with the brewery and the distillery. We've lost the early evening crowd and only have the late-night customers." The distillery serves fancy cocktails, but they are limited to two to a customer per day and they aren't open after eight. The brewery has the same guidelines for glasses of beer. I meet my friends at both places occasionally and, now that I thought about it, I hadn't been in a bar since Christmastime, right after the parade.

"I was the one who suggested looking into it," I admitted.

"What? Really?"

"The chief said he needed more money and another officer partly because of alcohol and drug abuse. The bars are only closed three hours a day. That seemed absurd to me."

Christy said that her regulars don't arrive until after ten or eleven, and that she often doesn't close until five if a few are still at the bar watching TV or playing pool.

"What good happens in a bar at that hour?"

"At least they are safe. I have trained bartenders. It's better than having them on the street. Then you'd have real problems instead of imaginary ones."

I did not bring up the bar hours again. Instead, the assembly considered putting a different question to the voters: should we levy an additional 2 percent sales tax on all retail alcohol sales and the newly legal marijuana sales? The intent would be to use the funds raised to help pay for police, recreational activities as healthy alternatives, and mental health and counseling programs to hopefully curb abuse. There were residents who testified that we should also tax sugar and sugary drinks since they do more harm than pot. Then the discussion became one about taxes being punitive, or judgmental, and pretty soon some people were saying that we should all only pay for the services we use, which became a junior high civics lesson on supporting the common good. Taxes are never popular, but we need them to pay for services. That's why I've been fine with placing tax questions on the ballot, whenever we can. The voters can choose if an alcohol or pot tax is fair.

Sometimes a preemptive action can appear to sort out a compromise. For instance, during the budget cycle the museum board may request a budget higher than it absolutely needs because they are assuming that they will likely receive 5 percent less. They are not being sneaky, but rather adjusting to a situation created by the budget hawks who have targeted cultural institutions even though they bring federal and state pass-through funds into our town. To some conservatives, the nuts and bolts of government spending are not as critical as a quote in the paper declaring that the fat has been trimmed from the budget and, see, everyone will survive, even the museum. Then they can say, "Told you so."

AS AN ASSEMBLY member I serve as the liaison to the planning commission; since I had been on it, I knew how it worked and could explain their decisions to the assembly, and the assembly's actions to them. The planning commission did not ask me, as liaison, if the assembly would overrule the permit they granted Roger Schnabel to move rocks from his land through a neighborhood and down to the harbor in order to both help fill in the beach before construction of the new parking lot, and expand an RV park he owns down there. If they had, then I could have warned them about what they were up against.

When Roger applied for what's called a conditional use permit—a permit for temporary but potentially disruptive activity—to allow him to haul rocks from a site behind a quiet residential neighborhood and down to the harbor, the planning commissioners gave Roger pretty much an unconditional pass to do what he wanted to do. It was more than he had even asked for, but he was happy to accept, as it would make his work easier and less costly. But when the neighborhood got wind of Roger's plans, hillside residents filed a formal appeal. They did not want any blasting, trucks, or additional traffic. They asked that the decision be overruled by the assembly, which has the authority to do so, and that Roger find his rocks for the project elsewhere. Some opponents cited previous permits for similar activities that they felt Roger's drivers had not followed. The hearings to settle the dispute marked a watershed moment for me. I had run on a campaign of "Community First," which to me meant residents' wishes were given equal or more weight than business interests. This sounded so simple. Turns out it wasn't.

The mayor was away for the hearing, so Mike, as her deputy mayor, took over. But he struggled to read the agenda and the packet. You may remember that Mike is in his eighties. He is nearly blind and it has been hard to witness his eyesight failing him. Whenever we've talked about making the assembly chambers comply with the Americans with Disabilities Act, we've focused on bathrooms and wheelchair access. A visual impairment should not prevent anyone from serving on the assembly, though, and the technology does exist to assist them. But Mike, like a lot of seniors, including my neighbor Betty, doesn't identify as someone needing special accommodations and so has not pressed the matter. Of course, the rest of us can see that Mike can't see and haven't intervened. Meetings come so quickly, there doesn't seem to be enough time to be proactive. All we do as an assembly is react.

The assembly chambers was full of people from the hillside neighborhood, as well as Roger's employees and fellow local business owners. Mike, who was frustrated after the first few moments of trying to read the procedural instructions out loud, asked Margaret if she would chair the meeting instead of him. She looked shocked and put her face in her hands. "Me? No. Yes. Okay." It would have been a challenge for anyone to run the unusually packed hearing. Margaret is the rare person who is introverted yet confident and steady under pressure. She does not seek the spotlight at all, but she rose to the occasion, leaning on her strong grasp of the Code and faith in the rule of law. Her father was an attorney.

As usual, my ties to so many of the people on both sides of the issue were tugging me in all different directions. Roger is my husband's hunting partner, and our daughter JJ's godfather. Nancy, his wife, is president of the Hospice of Haines board and I'm vice president. We have all been close friends for decades. One of the lead critics of the planning commission decision to issue the permit, Lenise Henderson-Fontenot, was also an old friend. She had written up and presented the appeal to the assembly. My daughter Sarah babysat Lenise's twin sons, Patrick and Royal, when she was in high school. Now Sarah, her husband, and their two young children live on a road that will be impacted by Roger's dump truck traffic. So do my sister, many friends, and members of my book club. One friend who lives there has an old dog that is particularly sensitive to fireworks. I can only imagine how blasting with dynamite, as Roger was planning to do to break up the rock he needed from his cliffy property, would affect the touchy terrier. The poor thing might dive out a window and never be seen again.

The meeting lasted three days. Yes, days. We began Tuesday night at 6:30, recessed at 10:00, resumed Wednesday afternoon from 1:00 to 5:30, and finally concluded Friday afternoon at about 4:00, in what the radio reported was the longest Haines Borough Assembly meeting on record. We did not convene on Thursday because the mayor was returning to town on the ferry, and Margaret was leaving for a vacation and would be en route. However, I spent a good part of that day studying the Code, reading the borough lawyer's brief and the appeal grounds again, and weighing those against the testimony we'd already heard. The mayor would be available Friday and Margaret agreed to call in from the Seattle airport during her long layover. We still needed Margaret's leadership to continue where we had left off and to guide us and the returning mayor on the finer points of the case in order to find an acceptable solution for everyone.

The time it all took was brutal, and the sacrifice it required was extreme. This might be a good place to explain some facts about life as a Haines assembly member. The whole assembly officially meets every other Tuesday night, and as a committee of the whole, or COW (as in having a COW, which always gets a laugh), about one Tuesday a month. The latter is typically a more informal gathering of the entire (thus "whole") assembly, where we discuss topics that may be on future agendas, or hear from the manager on issues of concern, but don't take any action. There are also other committees of the assembly, and committees and commissions that are advisory to the assembly, that convene regularly and that we often attend because we have to, or need to in order to be more well-informed.

Some weeks there are as many as seven meetings in five nights when they are scheduled back to back, such as a finance committee meeting at 5:30, and an assembly COW at 6:30. The budget season requires extra meetings, as do significant new hires, what with interviews and meet-and-greets for the job candidates. In other words, it's a big time commitment on a normal week.

No wonder Tom was howling that he had a newspaper to publish. (Even though he promised voters he would sell the paper or hire someone to run it if he were elected, that had proven, like many campaign promises, easier said than done.) And I know what he's like on a normal deadline. He must have had no sleep at all that week. Tresham missed the art classes he was supposed to teach, and Mike, who caught a bad cold, had a hard time staying alert for the duration. Margaret's voice was on the speakerphone in front of the mayor, but the rest of her was at a gate at SeaTac. I'm sure she hadn't planned to begin her vacation this way. Boarding announcements floated up into the meeting every now and then. As for myself, it was during that hearing that I realized that I may not be able to be a writer and an assemblywoman. The two vocations are not complementary unless you are a political commentator, but I don't write for the op-ed section.

In previous contentious votes that had been split 3–3 and the mayor had broken the tie (always on the side I wasn't on), there had been some bitter debates. In hindsight, I believe this was because the newer members of the group, myself included, were not as open to compromise as the senior assembly members were. We were not going to budge from our positions but insisted the other side should. Changing the world begins with the true believers, but I've learned that it is accomplished by the negotiators. In *Atlas Shrugged* Ayn Rand wrote that there is a right and wrong side to every issue and any middle ground is "always evil." Well, she never had to figure out how to move some rock from a mountain down a hill to the harbor with a minimum impact on the homes and families along its route.

For those three days we listened, asked questions, and I believe were fair and even kind to everyone who spoke from the crowd for and against Roger's permit. I tried to keep an open mind. It was emotional. Fathers were worried about their children's safety. Mothers were upset that they may not be able to enjoy summer days in the yard due to dust and noise. Roger and his crew took offense at the assumptions that they didn't care and wouldn't be considerate of the neighborhood families. When one parent pointed out that there were dogs and children in the road, a man from the other side of town said too bad, roads are for trucks and they should keep better track of kids and pets. Voices were raised, and there were some tears. My own daughter Sarah was not happy with me. Neither was my sister, and Roger wasn't, either. I would have preferred Roger had used another source for the rock, but he hadn't, and our job now was to find a solution.

In the end, the assembly worked with the borough staff to come up with a compromise. We accepted the planning commission's decision to allow the rock to be moved and the trucks to operate, but shortened the duration of the permit to months rather than a year, with limited hours on weekdays, and no trucking on the weekends or holidays. There was a safety plan to be approved by all parties, and dust and noise mitigation. We used our town's guiding documents, the Charter and the Code, as well as state law and our attorney's advice to make our ruling, and we kept our arguments to the law, rather than individuals, and better still: the assembly voted for it unanimously. The planning commission was not happy, but we had found a remedy to the problem their decision had created.

As we all stood packing up our papers and iPads, Tom declared loudly (he speaks in a shout as a rule), "Democracy! It's glorious chaos!"

"Exactly!" agreed Alekka Fullerton, the deputy clerk, who had been taking minutes because Clerk Cozzi was at a doctor's appointment in Juneau. There had been twists and turns, both legal and practical, and with each one we had backed up, taken a closer look, remedied the problem, and moved forward. You bet it took forever, and yes it was at times a zoo in those meetings, but Tom was right, out of the chaos came something glorious.

I was relieved to see Lenise and Roger chatting amicably as they left the chambers. They would meet the following week to finalize the safety plan with Brad. I also knew none of those three were completely happy with our decision or the amount of time we took to make it. It had been exhausting and less than ideal for us, as well. But everyone on the assembly was in a good mood now that it was over, because we had worked hard and done something right, to the best of our ability, in a tense setting. We had performed as leaders should. I really believed that.

But as I was gathering up my things I heard Tom ask Lenise's neighbor how he thought we had done. Joe's house was on the proposed truck route, at the sharpest corner of the dirt road. One year he planted apple trees all over town in an optimistic gesture I appreciated. Some even survived the winter. When he called me to ask for help on this issue, I said I would. I thought we had. Now Joe said he was dismayed and "very, very disappointed." He pointed at me. "Especially in you. Your daughter lives on that road." He said he wouldn't want to be me when an out-of-control truck ran over one of my grandchildren.

Caroline or Ivy? Really? Is that all he could say to me? My eyes stung. I was tired. I couldn't speak. My diamond tiara had turned to rust. I pulled on my heavy coat and mittens, lifted the backpack in which I haul assembly documents back and forth from home, and walked silently out of the hall to my car.

The story of how we shape our common existence, the rules that guide us, and the representatives who create them and to some extent ensure we abide by them, has some dazzling chapters—and they often contain pleasant surprises—but there are a lot of heartbreaking plot twists along the way. Please don't take this the wrong way. I believe that if we citizens, we voters—and we elected officials—acknowledge this truth, our democracy will be healthier. I hate to sound like a grandmother, but I am one, and so my dears, learn to share, take turns, and understand not everyone can have everything she wants all the time. Finally, and this may be the most important thing I will ever say about politics and life: accept apologies that won't be offered and forgive people who may never ask you to.

Manager and Committee Reports

State Park Ranger Travis Russell presented an update on a grant proposal to rehabilitate the Seduction Point Trail to Parks & Rec. He asked for a letter of support and received one.

Parks & Rec unanimously requests that the assembly create a long-term comprehensive plan for present and future winter recreation in Haines Borough.

A wastewater transmission line froze at the ferry terminal and we have supplied temporary septic holding tanks until flow returns to the line.

The borough manager's position is currently being advertised.

The Tourism Advisory Board has voted to change the name from "Haines Convention and Visitor's Bureau" to "Visit Haines."

NINE

It's Not Quitting Time

BETH CALLS OUR walks-and-talks "therapy." Without our mornings together, especially after meetings, I don't know if I would survive the assembly. But it's also a conversation about all her cares, since she is the hospice administrator and on the board of the assisted living home and is always, it seems, surrounded by people who rely on her for their well-being, in a different and lot less public way than they do me. I like having a friend who is political enough to pay attention to Rachel Maddow and agree with me on national stories but isn't particularly interested in the minutiae of assembly issues and so doesn't pressure me to take positions one way or the other.

Beth was moving ahead with her goal of turning her home and property into a healing arts center. She already has a meditation building and there are yoga yurts for summer workshops taught by a friend of hers from San Francisco. Beth's husband, Gregg, a commercial fisherman and a musician, hosts weekly music potlucks on the beach in front of their house all summer long, and recently they built a lodge that can accommodate her wellness retreats and his parties. It may be the only retreat center in the world that has a craps table in the freshly sage-smudged gathering hall.

One morning as we walked, I learned that they were almost ready to leave for a trip to Las Vegas so Gregg could visit the casinos and Beth could meet up with her sisters, who are ranchers, for a rodeo. Beth thought I'd like Las Vegas. Cirque du Soleil, George Strait (I know all the words to "Amarillo by Morning") and it's a great place to people watch because "the sidewalks are full of walking stories," she said. Beth is a vegetarian, cuts her own hair, and is handy with a chainsaw. Her coat has a duct-taped patch on it to keep the down from falling out. I was having trouble visualizing her at the MGM Grand.

"What will you wear?"

"Anything. There are people in jeans and in evening gowns." She said she had a tailored cowboy shirt for the rodeo.

The bitter cold and wind forced us to hike loops on the icy woodland trail adjacent to the beach, where the spruce trees block the gales. I told Beth about the latest crisis in local government. Every week, it seems, there was something that some residents resisted or supported as if it were a matter of life and death. The big house at the end of the road can't become a vacation rental. It will ruin the neighborhood! If the property can't be used that way, then the owners may subdivide it, and there could be six new homes blocking the views! Hunters say mountain goats will disappear if we allow heli-skiers into their territory, and the heli-ski guides snap back that hunters shoot goats, helicopters don't!

I'm still on a mission to make public meetings more civil (without preaching, as I've learned) but it is challenging, especially in January and February when the holidays are over and it's dark and cold and a long way to spring. There is time to stew on old and new beefs, especially for seasonal construction workers and fishermen. Cabin fever, Seasonal Affective Disorder, whatever you call it, is real. If you've noticed that I put a lot of emphasis on the weather, just know that the environment matters in Alaska. The winter blues must be acknowledged. They change people's judgment and can make us irrational. At a meeting about mapping the trails that cross-country skiers and snow-machiners both use, one of the snow-machiners, a large white man who also owns an airplane and just sold a fifty-four-foot boat, said he was concerned that snow machines would be prohibited from some ski trails. Without any hint of irony, he said that he was compelled to defend himself before it was too late, and by the same motivation Rosa Parks had when she refused to sit in the back of the bus.

"He compared himself to Rosa Parks?" Beth said. "No way."

"Beth, I'm not kidding. Everyone has lost their minds."

We trudged through a treeless gap in silence, ducking to keep our faces out of the bitter wind. Beth was not her usual self. She walked slower. Her shoulders sagged. I was being a lousy friend, all blah blah blah borough banter. When we finally were back in the stillness of the woods, I apologized. "I'm sorry to vent about meetings. What's going on with you?"

She sighed and said that the report from our friend Stephanie's biopsy was not good. The former mayor and my trusted advisor had been waiting for news of the results of surgery on a possible brain tumor. "It's not public yet, so this is under the dome," Beth said. "It's a glioblastoma," I think she said. "Whatever it is, it's bad." The doctors took out most of it during the biopsy, but they couldn't be certain given its type and size, and now predicted that Stephanie, who is seventy, had six months to seven years to live, depending on how the tumor and her body responded to their recommended treatments. "She's already reading a book on how to have a good death," Beth said. She was worried Stephanie might choose not to take the doctor's advice, that she might skip the drugs, chemotherapy, and radiation. Beth had hospice clients who had made that decision after such a diagnosis.

I didn't want to voice what I feared. I didn't want to assume the worst. "People get better even without treatment. It happens," I said.

We continued a little farther. "What would you do if you had a brain tumor?" Beth asked. "Would you try to beat it or walk away from the hospital and go home?"

I don't have a bucket list. I like my life as it is. Would I alter anything if I were hiking in Stephanie's boots? It would be strange not to, wouldn't it? Then again, wouldn't the bravest and most optimistic choice when facing death be to live the way I always had, only with new conviction and tenderness because I knew that it wouldn't last much longer? The few times in my life when I had been laid low by injuries, I had time to watch hummingbirds hover in the geraniums and talk to my friends without checking my watch. There were blessings in the downtime. Still, I didn't just give up. This was different, though. And it was *her* brain, *her* life, not mine. Surely, though, there was a middle ground?

I told Beth that if it were me, I would give the cancer treatments a try. I listed the people living with cancer that we know, and the ones who have been healed and are in remission. But I'm twelve years younger than Stephanie, ten years younger than Beth. "And I would hope I'd make a few significant lifestyle changes," I said.

"I bet I know one," Beth said.

• • •

WE DID NOT hire Brad as permanent manager. We chose Debra Schnabel instead, following a series of public interviews with residents, borough staff, and the assembly. There had been a petition asking us to give the position to Brad, and Big Don supported him, as did many others who wrote and spoke in his favor. My daughter Sarah and her husband. My younger neighbors. Stephanie had written in support of Debra, as had many of my women friends. It was an open secret that should Brad *not* be selected, the recall petitions would surface and the campaign to oust me and Tom would begin in earnest. The assembly's task was to choose the most qualified candidate. Debra had a master's in public administration, and she had served on the old city council and the committee that wrote the Borough Charter. She answered the questions in the interviews in ways that made my heart sing. The meeting in which we chose her was packed with Brad's supporters, and some of Debra's.

In my mind, we were getting two local candidates who could almost be co-managers. (We had eliminated an out-of-town finalist following a phone interview.) It made sense to make Debra the manager and have Brad as her sort of co-manager, as he would remain in charge of facilities and oversee the Public Works department, and be paid the same as she was. Turns out this semi-shared position theory made things harder. Mike had supported Brad. Before that deciding meeting adjourned, Mike stood up, and as he had done several times before, put on his hat, brandished his cane, and said goodnight. Only this time he announced he would not be back. He quit. He wished us good luck and left. Now we needed to replace Mike, as the assembly makes the appointments until the next regular election, which was not until October, an entire spring and summer away.

By then Stephanie had decided to try chemotherapy. However, she chose to have her treatments at the small Juneau cancer clinic rather than the major medical center in Seattle that her doctor had encouraged her to go to. She planned to wait until the following fall to travel back down to Washington for a follow-up and another MRI. While cancer isn't contagious, it appeared that quitting might be. After Mike left, the assistant harbormaster did, as well. He said he couldn't keep working for eighteen dollars an hour with two children to support. He had hoped to be promoted if Brad moved up to the permanent manager job and the harbormaster took Brad's old position in charge of borough facilities—but things hadn't gone that way. The tourism director quit, too, and the administrative assistant to the manager authored a commentary published in the newspaper berating us all, and then announced her resignation would take effect after the paid vacation she was owed. Next the assembly received two more public records requests for all emails to and from assembly members regarding Debra. Margaret balked at turning over Debra's recipe for ginger-carrot cake. "I promised her I'd keep it a secret," she said. The attorney agreed that it did not constitute a public document.

While we all have borough email addresses and keep official borough business off our personal emails, sometimes it crosses over, especially with friends whose email addresses pop up automatically. Hillary had her own server; we have computers, phones, and an iPad that doesn't always distinguish between them. Which means we all have to be super vigilant, but even so, I would have my own issues soon enough and be accused of violating the open meeting laws in an email correspondence with Tresham. This became so stressful that for a while I stopped emailing as an assembly member altogether. Whenever I received an email message, I'd either talk to the sender in person or call them up. Sometimes it was only to say thank you. It was easier than sorting through everything later.

In addition to all the resignations there was Big Don and Co.'s constant drumbeat for recall. Ryan Cook had run and lost in the previous election and had been fueling the discontent in his closed Rant & Rave Facebook group for months. The pro-recall people conducted their campaign to oust us—the new and liberal assembly members who now were in the majority—mainly on the Rant & Rave page, so anyone who was not a "friend" could not see what was said and circulated. Among their grievances were the firing of the first manager, our views on the harbor, of course the mine and timber sales: We were too green, overruling the planning commission, supporting the library and the pool. We weren't pro-business, and we spent too much money. They objected to our looking into ways to make the town more bike-friendly. Everything we did, or said, or wanted to do, and even didn't say or do, was up for comment and review. Hiring Debra was the last straw.

This was all taking a toll on the assembly's health. I had a cold I couldn't shake, and I never get sick. Tom looked terrible. His face was gray and his voice scratchy when he showed up one day around noon at my house, declined tea, but accepted some orange juice and helped himself to a banana. Then he plopped down on the window seat with his boots and coat still on, and closed his eyes. I thought he was asleep. With his eyes shut he said all he wanted to do was go home to his cabin, but he couldn't because his small fleet of rusted old rigs was falling apart. "I don't even have a truck with four-wheel drive right now."

Slowly, though, things improved as we began to anticipate the annual miracle of summer, which makes Alaskans forget winter, the way some women do childbirth. I knew that soon my cherry trees would bloom, and the wind died down and the sky turned blue as Beth and I walked down the path to the beach again a few weeks after we hired Debra. "What if this is the last spring I have on earth?" Beth said. Her knees had been bothering her, and her back from prepping her garden, and she said she had a bump on her nose she worried could be melanoma, but I couldn't see it (she has a lot of freckles).

"Well, at least it would have been a nice one. What a day."

DESPITE THE BETTER weather, Stephanie, who has studied Buddhism, meditation, and yoga, and who is very, very intelligent, and reads all kinds of philosophy texts, seemed to be struggling with how to fill her days meaningfully now that her treatments were over. We all are terminal—everyone dies—but some of us have a better idea about when exactly that might be. Stephanie had been told for her it was between one and five years. I couldn't imagine how scary that must be. It's not something a person can comprehend until it happens. I thought Stephanie was joking when she floated the idea of her filling Mike's term until October. Who would want to jump into this mess now? Right as the recall seemed to be heating up?

As we walked on another day, I admitted to Beth that I wouldn't spend what could be my last summer ever at assembly meetings in this town right now, that's for sure. "It's not worth it." I said.

"Then why haven't you quit?"

"It's not so easy to live each day as if it were your last." I had obligations. I thought I was making a difference. Hiring Debra was a good decision and I stood by it even if Mike didn't.

"Stephanie loves government. She loves education," Beth said.

"Stress is bad for cancer. Being on the assembly is making Tom sick and he's healthy."

"It's not up to you to decide what is good or bad for Stephanie," Beth said.

She had a point. Beth was an expert in end-of-life issues. She knew that most terminally ill people she had cared for want life to be as normal as possible for as long as possible. "Stephanie thrives on the process of government," she said. "She loves it. Why not let her have that much?"

Anyway, it wasn't up to me. The assembly would make the decision as a group and there were other candidates who wanted the seat. There would be interviews and letters of intent to read. There was one young man who was campaigning with a petition full of signatures supporting him, with many of the same names who had objected to Debra's hire. Great. Big Don put his name in, too. Yes, this was an opportunity to reach out to the other side. To avert disaster. He wouldn't recall us if we chose him, would he? I had read *Team of Rivals*, too. But I was no Lincoln. Lately, I had been making Mary Todd look mellow. And Stephanie's qualifications were too good to be true. She was a former mayor, as was Mike, so her appointment would ensure we didn't lose that experience and that there would be no learning curve, which if mine was any indication, is steep. Cooper, Stephanie's furry orange dog, had been trained in emotional support and could attend meetings in his new vest and harness. Stephanie had written a letter endorsing Debra, so she would be a positive force in what was becoming a rocky transition for our new manager, and Stephanie and the mayor also got along well, and from my perspective that fence needed mending. Big Don even liked her, so if he didn't get Mike's seat—which was not going to happen and he likely knew it—there was that sprinkling of fairy dust, too.

You know how much I admire and rely on Stephanie for advice. So do many other people. She had a lot of champions. The meeting to decide was looming. Everyone knew she had brain cancer, but she made sure the specific details of her treatments and prognosis were kept private and upbeat. Mostly, she assured everyone she was well enough to do the job while she recovered from her first round of treatments, and that she wanted to. Besides, it was only for a few months. Just until the next regular election.

"Hold it," I said to Beth as we talked it out and walked. "This is crazy. I can't vote to appoint Stephanie. I mean, she has a brain tumor! As much as I would love to sit next to her, I can't support this precisely because she is my friend. Isn't cancer enough of an excuse to stay home and eat ice cream and literally stop and smell her flowers?"

"She's on a no-sugar diet. It apparently feeds cancer."

"Carrots then, whatever."

"It's her life, not yours," she said. "I think you should talk to her."

I drove out to Stephanie's little flower farm at Paradise Cove and we sat on the deck while I admired the view. A work party of friends and neighbors had trimmed some trees and prepared the grounds for the season, turning over beds and wheelbarrowing gravel for the paths, raking and clipping, and they even painted her window trim. The place looked great. Stephanie did, too. A bit frail, but she's small to begin with, and her hair had always been short. The colorful cap was pretty. I did my best to keep Cooper out of my lap, which was not easy. I bet he weighs more than Stephanie.

I told her that if I had a brain tumor, I'd quit the assembly. "It is probably giving me one," I half-joked.

Stephanie smiled and blinked behind her new glasses, new since her vision had changed after the brain surgery. She said she wanted to be useful, and it was clear that the assembly, and by extension our community, could use some assistance. She enjoyed public decision-making and it would help her keep her mind off her cancer and her doctor's evaluation that fall. She had no intention of running for the seat in the next election. She did not say so out loud, but we both understood her meaning. By then she might be too ill, by then she might not be as able to read and write, to speak and reason.

As gently as possible she asked, "Why do you believe you know what is best for me? I'm sure your friends and family didn't think you should ride a bike after your accident, but you love it, so you did. Right? I loved being on the assembly and being mayor. I'd like to do it again while I still can. Who are you to decide I shouldn't even be considered?" All she wanted from me was to treat her like all the other candidates and choose her if I believed she was the best person for the task. If the assembly decided on someone else, she said, "That's fine." Stephanie is the most cerebral of my friends. Local leadership was her exercise, her outlet, her recreation. She wanted to apply her wits and skills, her intuition and her education, to something other than her own condition. She wanted

her brain to fire on all those synapses that public service requires
while, as she said, it still could.

AFTER STEPHANIE WAS sworn in, we shuffled seats in
the assembly chambers. Debra chose my old position on the end,
and I moved in one seat, next to Stephanie who was at the mayor's
right hand where the former manager had sat. It already felt better tucked in there. I liked having Cooper under the table, and as
Stephanie predicted he was a perfect gentleman when he was on
duty. Stephanie had been a special education teacher for years. It's
a job that requires patience, problem-solving skills, and redefin-
ing success frequently. So does governing. Stephanie brought calm
and perspective to our meetings, and in a most welcome practical
matter, our concern for her health shortened them. It wasn't fair to
make her stay up too late. I believe her illness, while not spoken of,
influenced our decisions. Nothing we were doing would likely kill
us, or the community, but it all mattered enough that it was worth
Stephanie spending even her borrowed time on. It made what I
was doing more meaningful, and I sensed the mayor felt that way
as well. Jan had lost her husband to cancer. I was not surprised
when she appointed Stephanie as her new deputy mayor, which
also meant that Stephanie even ran some meetings again.

AND THEN MARGARET quit the assembly suddenly,
shortly after we hired Debra. I couldn't believe it, but she said wit-
nessing the vitriol and reading the vile comments on Rant & Rave
about the assembly in general and some aimed at her specifically
was incredibly upsetting. (While we all had been blocked, a few
sympathetic members sent her screen shots of the worst rants.)

She'd had it. She'd also hoped the mayor would have been more supportive of the whole assembly. Luckily, Margaret's seat was filled relatively easily with another young person like herself— Sean, who had two little kids and managed Dusty Trails, a low-income apartment complex a block from the assembly chambers, so he walked to the meetings. I envied him having Stephanie as a mentor for his first experience in office.

IN THE MEANTIME, Debra advertised for those recently vacated borough jobs and they were filled, except for the opening for her assistant, who after that vacation changed her mind and Debra forgave her, and now they, and we, are working together on a grant to upgrade the municipal building and assembly chambers to comply with the Americans with Disabilities Act.

When, a few months later, Stephanie returned from her exam in Seattle with what she said was shocking news, I braced myself. I had been reading all about brain cancer on the internet. It turned out that they couldn't find the tumor. Stephanie's cancer was gone. The doctors weren't even sure what had happened. They had not expected this. There was no clear explanation, except the obvious one that the cancer treatments worked. For now. There is always the possibility some too-tiny-to-see bits of the tumor remain and could grow again.

I sometimes wonder if I might have followed Mike and Margaret out the door if I hadn't had the opportunity to sit next to Stephanie and Cooper during those months soaking up their emotional support. Like when Stephanie would lean over and whisper, "Don't say anything" after some pointed public testimony by a critic, or during those times that I was frustrated with Tom. Even though we often agreed, when we didn't, he would be so convinced that he was right and I was wrong that he would keep on speaking to the issue, only louder, and longer. Then Stephanie would pass me a note—"Just vote"—and I would, and we'd move on, and it would be okay, and I'd find my voice again when I needed to use it. Stephanie reminded me to concentrate on each play and each inning, rather than focus on the scoreboard. She also said that if I didn't want to attend a particular meeting, I should skip it.

Not show up? Is that even allowed?

"You may have three unexcused absences," she said, and quoted the Code. "Go ahead and take one if you need to. You don't have to explain why. That is perfectly acceptable."

EVERYONE KNOWS THAT a terminal diagnosis clarifies priorities, but it doesn't change them completely. I'm currently reading *Faith: Trusting Your Own Deepest Experience* by Sharon Salzberg. Stephanie lent it to me. It can't be a coincidence that Salzberg teaches how living intentionally and doing what we can to contribute to the well-being of a community is life-changing, and perhaps life-saving.

I never have used my get-out-of-jail-free cards to avoid a meeting. Knowing that I can, though, has made all the difference. Cooper stays in the car now when Stephanie is inside the chambers. Stephanie has all the love she needs from the assembly, the mayor, and I dare say a grateful community. Although around here we don't voice those kinds of things out loud, except at funerals. Thank goodness there wasn't one.

Two years after we appointed Stephanie to the assembly, she is still healthy, and, since she chose to run for office that fall after all, still the deputy mayor. On a sunny morning as we walked, I asked Beth what she thought had really cured our friend's cancer. Was it meditation? Diet? The drugs? Could it have been divine? Beth said, without hesitation, "Being on the assembly healed her."

One evening a while later Stephanie stopped by on her way home to say hello just as I was preparing dinner. She declined a glass of wine, but pulled up a stool. I asked her if she thought being on the assembly so soon after that devastating diagnosis had been good medicine. "I needed a distraction. I couldn't think about cancer all the time and the assembly filled that need." She said while it had helped, and that even with the cancer supposedly gone, "I still think about it, and I dread the regular check-ups. It could come back. I am hoping that someday the worry will end, and I will learn to accept that possibility but not dwell on it." Then she brought up how upset Sean was at our last meeting over a couple of budget amendment proposals he disagreed with. "If Sean had said 'I quit,'" Stephanie said, "I might have been right behind him and out that door. The weather has been so beautiful, and my garden needs water, and I love my new lawn mower. I am weary of meetings."

So even Stephanie, for whom sitting on the assembly had literally been death-defying, sometimes still finds the task we do so maddening that she contemplates resigning.

But she didn't and she won't. And I hope no one else does.

Manager and Committee Reports

Spring tour guide training will be at the museum. The Tourism Advisory Board has asked if bear encounter training is, or should be, included for the Chilkoot corridor tour operators.

Two meetings were held regarding police service outside the townsite now that the state has removed the trooper post. The general sentiment from the community is that they want emergency police response but not patrols, and that they pay enough taxes and should not have to pay more for emergency service. The big question is, "What is emergency service?"

National Public Radio booked the Chilkat Center conference room for eight hours. The center also hosted a cello and violin concert.

Deputy Clerk Alekka Fullerton is currently enrolled in a two-week course at the Northwest Clerks Institute. Clerk Julie Cozzi is back after a week's leave.

TEN

Recall, Part One

ALASKA'S RECALL LAW allows for any elected official to be recalled after 120 days in office on the grounds of "misconduct in office, incompetence, or failure to perform prescribed duties." The standard that the local clerk uses to certify a recall petition is that the claims are *possible*, not whether any are *true*. The law empowers citizens—first the petition signers and then the voters in a special election—to determine if an official should be recalled for the stated causes.

On April 12, now-former clerk Julie Cozzi granted Don Turner Jr.'s request to circulate petitions to recall me from the office of Haines Borough Assembly Member for misconduct in office. Big Don is officially Don Turner Jr. and used his full name for this very official act. (His son Donnie is Don Turner III.) Assemblymen Tom Morphet and Tresham Gregg were also petitioned for recall. Big Don asked that more passers, or petitioners, be sworn in to gather the signatures, and the clerk complied by providing them with petitions as well.

The passers had sixty days to convince a minimum of 258 registered voters to agree with them that a special election should be held for the purposes of recalling us. Two hundred and fifty-eight is 25 percent of the 1,032 voters in the previous regular election. That's the one that Tom and I won, mind you. Tresham was already on the assembly, but had another year to go, so they figured they might as well be rid of all three of us liberals. The law requires a quarter of all voters to sign on to the charges, making recall of small-town officials easier than those in larger cities or the Alaska State Legislature, just by virtue of the numbers. In the upcoming summer and fall there would also be assembly recall attempts in the Alaskan towns of Petersburg, Homer, and not long afterward, Unalaska. Petersburg's was dismissed before it began, as the clerk determined the grounds were flimsy, and Homer and Unalaska's special elections both failed to recall anyone.

In Kyle Clayton's news summary of 2017, my annus horribilis as the Queen would say, he treated the drama of the recall clinically, with a minimum of invasive procedures. "A shake-up in leadership across government and business, a group of unsatisfied citizens who challenged the assembly and how to approach policing outside the townsite dominated the news this year." It only took Kyle one sentence to tell the story that I am going to write pages and pages about.

Tom had hired Kyle, an army medic who served in Iraq, to run the *Chilkat Valley News* when he couldn't sell it as readily as he had hoped but still needed to fulfill his campaign promise to cut ties with the paper. After the army, Kyle attended journalism school. He's in his early thirties with dusty red hair and a sweet smile. In June, as the recall campaign heated up, Kyle would buy the paper outright from Tom.

As it turned out, the newspaper played a part in the recall. The evidence, as set forth on the recall petition, alleged that Tom and I misused our positions on the assembly for personal gain when we asked the police chief to put the police blotter back in the newspaper after the chief decided it was not necessary. The daily log of police calls and responses had been published weekly seemingly forever. The same new police chief who decided it wasn't necessary had also forwarded a misconstrued criminal complaint against me and other assembly members to the Juneau District Attorney, who promptly dismissed it. The recall petition accused Tom, Tresham, and me of violating Alaska's open meetings law because of an email Tresham had sent to me. Tom argued all along that there was no evidence against him in it, and that it should have been thrown out. To this day, I don't understand how the borough attorney, the one we rely on from his office in Anchorage, and the clerk ruled that Tom could be guilty by association.

There was a lot more to the saga than emails and a police blotter. Hiring Debra instead of Brad motivated some residents to sign the recall election petition who may not have otherwise. Big Don, for one, disagreed with our decision. This is an understatement worthy of Joe "Just the facts, ma'am" Friday. But Brad and Debra worked well together. She had won over the staff, and I considered her appointment a highlight of my time in office, even if it did fuel the final push for signatures on my recall petition.

The co-sponsor of the recall was Ryan of Rant & Rave, one of the candidates Tom and I had defeated in the last election, and most of the recall campaign was conducted on that closed Facebook group. The recall proponents also wrote some public letters to the editor calling us self-serving, unfit for office, a vocal minority, and mentioning just about every grievance they had with assembly decisions or actions since we were elected in October—including some that were pure fiction. One signer told me that our insane program to buy hundred-dollar water meters for every household in town gave him no choice but to oust us. We had never even discussed water meters. Another recall supporter came to one of our meetings and asked the entire assembly to resign in order to start fresh with the right people.

Margaret had already quit the assembly and now, as a civilian, she rose to our defense by chairing the anti-recall campaign, which placed ads in the paper and put up signs. Under Margaret's leadership, the anti-recall group focused not on personalities or divisiveness, or even on engaging with the other side, but rather on what they characterized as a misuse of the recall process to have an election "do-over," as well as on the insincerity of the evidence against us.

Tom roared back at the recall challenge, swinging hard in every direction. The police especially felt his wrath over what he deemed a misuse of their power, and the union representing the police filed a grievance—statewide, union leaders urged that Tom be recalled. The assembly censured him because he went too far by criticizing officers by name.

Tresham, on the other hand, was not bothered a bit. He said he had never been more energized to do good work or felt so much love from so many people. "Heather," he said to me when I confessed I was miserable, "it's not about you. It is about them. This says much more about their souls than it does ours." Tresham meditates a lot.

MEANWHILE, KYLE WAS considering whether or not to buy the paper and commit to the town—the *Chilkat Valley News* is vital to our well-being—he clearly was smitten by Haines but wary of being jilted. The petitions had begun to be circulated and he could see what was happening to three people who had spent their lives devoted to Haines in various ways. It was hard to believe I had once been the grand marshal of the parade, the Chamber of Commerce volunteer-of-the-year, the lauded hometown author. Now I was embarrassed to appear at the grocery store and I had already stopped attending high school basketball games months before. I averted my eyes from Ryan's truck parked so visibly and, it seemed, in every prominent location, its giant recall sign displaying my name propped up in the back.

The last thing I wanted was for Kyle not to have the opportunity for the kind of life I had in Haines. Until recently, it had been great. Over coffee at a back table at Mountain Market, I admitted to Kyle that when I walked into the borough office now it felt like the floor was covered in snakes. I didn't trust anyone anymore. The proof of my perfidy, and thus the legal reason to even hold a recall election, was an email the police chief had sent to the interim manager (that would be Brad) months earlier alleging that by my asking him to consider putting the blotter back in the paper (because residents like to know what the police are doing, and it reassures us to know how responsive the local officers are to everything from a bear tipping over the school dumpster to finding a lost cell phone) I had misused my authority.

What was odd was that I had never been called into the office and reprimanded, or even informed that the chief felt this way— by him or Brad or anyone. But Big Don must have known about it, because in a public records request he had asked the clerk for that specific email. If the chief's complaint were valid, and I had broken the law, why had no one censured me at the time, the way the assembly had censured Tom when he'd stepped over a line?

There were ten petitions circulated by Don's crew. Nine men and one woman kept them on clipboards in their trucks, carried them into bars and stores, and knocked on doors saying who knows what about me, hoping for a signature. Thank God for my early morning bike rides with Chip. Even when I'd toss and turn all night, he'd nudge me out of bed at five for his version of marriage therapy. He knows that I will always be okay as long as I sweat hard and deeply breathe in the solace of open spaces, as Gretel Ehrlich wrote. She survived a lightning strike. I survived the news that Big Don and his partners had filed completed, i.e., signed, petitions. But barely. Two hundred and seventy-four Haines residents had concluded that I should be recalled for misconduct in office, or at least they were in favor of putting it to the people for a vote. The first four signatures on the petition were former Haines manager Bill Seward and his wife, Cary, who apparently were still registered to vote here even though they were long gone; Diana, who had run for assembly against me and lost; and Don. The crappy crabber was one of the petition passers.

WHEN I HEARD the news on the radio that the clerk had certified the petitions, my stomach dropped. At least I was home and not at Mountain Market. Julie Cozzi had promised to tell us when the petitions were turned in before she spoke to the media, as a courtesy, like notifying the next of kin in an accidental death, but she hadn't. When I ran in to complain, she said she had been too busy. The mayor said she forgot, too, and shrugged. I stumbled out of the office and headed back to the safety of my house.

Chip was washing the dinner dishes and I was still at the table sipping wine when the phone rang. "If it's for me, I'm not here," I said. I could not bear sympathy. I had only glanced at the petitions that were posted on the borough website and what I had seen made me want to flee to Tenakee with Teresa. It was humiliating. He handed me the phone anyway, because it was my sister. Suzanne asked how I was doing, and I said, "Oh, you know, just great. I've had a wonderful day. Actually, not so hot."

"It's awful," she said. "I'm really sorry." She pulled up my petition on her screen and commenced to read the names. Not all 274. Which, by the way, was sixteen more than required. The signatories included more of my peers than there are children in our entire school, grades K–12. She didn't read the names we knew would be there. She read the people who knew me well and still chose to endorse Big Don's version of my sins, and even worse, never took the trouble to ask me if they were true.

I told my sister that I had closed the PDF file after seeing the name of one of the residents at Haines Assisted Living, where I volunteer. She is a funny old woman whom I visit whenever I stop in. I didn't think she even knew I was *on* the borough assembly. She may not even remember what the borough assembly is. Someone talked her into it.

Suzanne couldn't believe my golfing partner signed it. "Weren't they at your house for Christmas dinner?" That name I had spotted already, and I'd called her up right away. She said she was sorry, but that when I took the mayor's paycheck away while the mayor was at the hospital with her aging mother in the ICU, that was the last straw. It was cruel, she said. How could I do such a thing?

The question was how could she believe that I would ever do such a thing? Is that what Don told her?

I explained that no one took any money away from the mayor. We had lowered the salary for the *next* mayor's term because the current figure was thousands of dollars higher than any town our size in Alaska, and we were looking at ways to balance the budget, which is something her side—I'm assuming what side she's on— always supports. The mayor will still be paid $7,000 a year, and that's double what the assembly gets. Talking to her did no good, though. I only upset her more.

As I spoke with Suzanne now, Chip kept doing the dishes and glancing over to monitor my emotional temperature. Suzanne kept scanning her screen and reeling off names. Two of the bank tellers. The butcher. A nurse at the clinic who had tended Betty when I brought her in for that cut on her head.

I was sitting at my dining table, our mother's old table, the antique one that was in the house Suzanne and I grew up in and I'd had shipped to Alaska to help make this house feel like home. My sister had followed me to Haines, and met and married her husband here. My niece grew up in their bed-and-breakfast up the hill on Officers Row in Fort Seward. Our other sister still lives back east near our dad. He loves to follow Haines news with his subscription to the paper. What will he think when he reads about my fall from grace? Have I let him down, too?

Suzanne continued to name names. "Who's that?" she asked of one signatory.

"He built our house," I told Suzanne.

"His wife signed it, too. How come?"

"I don't know."

Then she read my fisherman friend Stuart's name. He had told me he was going to sign it because we'd hired Debra instead of his friend Brad. At the time, even though we had disagreed, we had hugged after the meeting. "It's a long story," I told Suzanne. "And complicated." It was becoming difficult to breathe and my heart was ping-ponging off my ribs.

"Why would all these people sign this?" Suzanne asked. She was concerned with the why and how of it all. I just saw faces, children, gardens, weddings, funerals, trucks, and even dogs. Big Don was persuasive. He had tailed a friend of mine home and pleaded with him to sign it. (He didn't.) Apparently Don's method was to assure people, like my friend, that their signature wouldn't mean they favored recalling me, only that they supported the democratic process. Voting was always a good thing, right? So more voting was always better, right? Except that wasn't correct. A signature on this petition meant the signer attested that the evidence against me was true and that I should be recalled in a special election because I had committed misconduct in office.

Suzanne read another name. "I thought he liked you."

Me, too. He used to race bikes with us.

I speculated that a lot of these people were probably mortified that the petition had been made public, especially if they'd signed it believing it was harmless. Or even that it was the good government thing to do. They couldn't have meant to hurt me or Chip or our family, I told Suzanne.

"Maybe they all don't," Suzanne said, "but the people behind the recall sure as hell do. They know exactly what they are doing."

It had been a long day. My face was a blotchy wet mess.

Suzanne is my little sister, and she hated to see me scorned, and she was going to confront the recall head on, person to person, if need be. With each new name, she was more incredulous, shocked, angry, and disgusted. The clerk's husband signed it, so did the police chief's wife, and the mayor's sisters, too. People for whom I'd personalized copies of my books, and had once valued my signature, had used theirs against me. A swimmer I talk with at the pool, a baker, a carpenter, a pilot . . .

Suzanne couldn't know that each name she read struck me like a stone. I am very good at pretending I'm tougher than I am. I couldn't tell her how I really felt because everything hurt so bad that I was afraid I would break if I tried to say too much.

. . . the friendly guy who plowed our driveway. Friends of our son. Friends of our daughters. Our granddaughter was a flower girl in one guy's son's wedding. We probably won't be invited to their big Fourth of July party anymore . . .

. . . the grocer.

This name, I repeated aloud.

Chip looked up from dish duty. "Really?" We were good customers of his store, and he of ours. He had even spoken up for us in one meeting, denouncing a boycott of our lumberyard that one of the recall sponsors was encouraging on Facebook. Now Chip looked stricken as he repeated his fellow merchant's name.

Next Suzanne named an old friend.

"Ed? Are you sure? That couldn't be our Ed." He had been Chip's goat hunting partner. He had taught Chip how, and Chip had helped the old man hunt in his later years, packing gear and cutting trails when it was too difficult for Ed to manage the steep slopes and heavy backpacks. Ed had polished the mountain goat horns on the wall in our kitchen. If Ed died before his dog did, I had promised we'd adopt him. "It can't be our Ed," I repeated.

Suzanne read the name again, confirming it was.

"Ed wouldn't recall me!" I wailed.

Chip wiped his hands on a towel and reached for the phone. "Time to hang up, Heath," he whispered. "This isn't doing anybody any good." He made an excuse to Suzanne and told her we'd talk tomorrow.

Then his face crumpled. I could see him registering the knowledge that all his goodwill and good deeds and hard work—staying open six days a week every week for over thirty years while advising builders, homeowners, and business people, all those sports teams and community events he'd sponsored, all the fundraisers he'd contributed to—hadn't mattered to nearly three hundred people. In a place this size, that's a lot. Those names on my petition were his customers and his friends. Will we be voted off this little town that might as well be an island?

Out the open door, the wild roses and cherry trees caught the breeze, the sun broke through the rolling clouds between the mountains and the river, shining on the inlet. Jesus rays, I call them. Our grandchildren played on the beach, Pearl barking after them. How could the end of the world be so beautiful?

HAINES BOROUGH OFFICIAL BALLOT SPECIAL ELECTION – AUGUST 15, 2017

PROPOSITION #1

"Shall Tresham Gregg be recalled from the office of borough assembly member?"

○ YES   NO ○

Grounds for Recall:

Violation of the open meeting act (AS 44.62.310). In a Dec. 12, 2016 email Morphet, Lende, Gregg, and Jackson communicating on the 33' harbor extension by email and/or phone. More than three assembly members cannot communicate outside of an official meeting about Borough business.

Response from Mr. Gregg:

When elected officials make decisions that we don't like, we can choose to not reelect them when their tenure is up. That's democracy. Recall elections are not for reversing decisions, they're for removing elected officials who have broken the law. State law prohibits the clerk from evaluating the recall allegations; you are being asked to decide if laws were broken, not whether you agree with every decision made.

Sending emails to other members expressing an opinion is not illegal; no law was broken. No decision was made outside of the open meeting. People are abusing the recall procedure to throw out recent election results that didn't go their way. That's unethical and expensive. Their requests for documents, staff and attorney time, and special election expenses cost this community thousands of dollars, and it divides the community further.

I am happy to talk to anyone in this community on any topic. We may not always agree, but I will keep trying my best to responsibly help manage the Borough's affairs, make our government more efficient, and keep important services happening that benefit people in the Chilkat Valley. Please vote no on this attempted recall.

||||||||||||||||||||||||||||||||||||||||||||||||||||||||||||||||||||||||||||||||||||||||||||||||||||||||||

PROPOSITION #2

"Shall Heather Lende be recalled from the office of borough assembly member?"

○ YES   NO ○

Grounds for Recall:

1. (HBC 2.06.030) misuse of official position

1/11/17 – Email to the manager, Police Chief Scott complained

"Based on last night's meeting as well as several other encounters (documented) I believe Assembly members Morphet and Lende require direction regarding requesting HBPD to provide the blotter." Coercion of a subordinate in an attempt to affect a personal or financial interest is misuse of her official position. The interest she has is she stand [sic] to benefit through her connection with the CVN newspaper and her personal blog.

2. Violation of open meeting act (AS 44.62.310)

12/12/2016 – Email Morphet, Lende, Gregg, and Jackson communicating on the 33' harbor extension by email and/or phone. More than three assembly members cannot communicate outside of an official meeting about Borough business.

Response from Ms. Lende:

Thank you for electing me to the assembly last October. I would like to continue working on your behalf for what's best for our community.

I trust you to know that I would never use my office for personal financial gain. I earn about a $1,000 a year writing obituaries for the Chilkat Valley News and that work is not connected to the police report, which is back in the paper anyway. I also did not conduct public business in private by receiving an email from a fellow assembly member asking me to vote against something I and the assembly voted for. One email from one assembly person to another is not violating any laws. Both charges are baseless, and now moot.

This recall isn't about the charges anyway, and you know that.

The real question is do you want to allow democracy to work in Haines, and let the people we elect serve out our terms, or do you want to encourage special interest groups to hijack elections through this flawed recall process? This election is about the soul of our wonderful town. Please affirm what's true and good about Haines and vote no on the recall.

||||||||||||||||||||||||||||||||||||||||||||||||||||||||||||||||||||||||||||||||||||||||||||||||||||||||

PROPOSITION #3
"Shall Tom Morphet be recalled from the office of borough assembly member?"

○ YES   NO ○

Grounds for Recall:

1. (HBC 2.06.030) misuse of official position

1/11/17 – Email to the manager, Police Chief Scott complained

"Based on last night's meeting as well as several other encounters (documented) I believe Assembly members Morphet and Lende require direction regarding requesting HBPD to provide the blotter." Coercion of a subordinate in an attempt to affect a personal or financial interest is misuse of his official position. The interest he has is he stands to benefit through his connection with the CVN newspaper and his personal blog.

2. Violation of open meeting act (AS 44.62.310)

12/12/2016 – Email Morphet, Lende, Gregg, and Jackson communicating on the 33' harbor extension by email and or phone. More than three assembly members cannot communicate outside of an official meeting about borough business.

Response from Mr. Morphet:

As someone with a longtime concern for our community, I urge you to vote "no" in today's recall election.

Haines has a history of vigorous civic debate. But the will of the people, as expressed in a legitimate election, should not be undone without substantive cause and careful consideration.

You may not be aware of the grounds for this recall, which do not meet that standard.

With regards to the police blotter, a record of police calls has been provided to the public—not only to the newspaper—for decades. Police had posted it for years on their Facebook page. I continue to support full public access to public records.

While my name was mentioned in an email sent by one fellow assembly member to another, I never received the e-mail in question. The email was not a group e-mail or chain e-mail. It was a single message from one assembly member to another. Neither I nor other assembly members violated the Open Meetings Act.

It's an honor to represent you on the Haines Borough Assembly. With due respect for the electoral process, I ask you to vote "no."

★ ELEVEN ★

Recall, Part Two

FOLLOWING STATE GUIDELINES, the election to recall Tom, Tresham, and me was set for nine weeks after the petitions were certified. Also by law, the assembly was required to declare a special Election Day for the purpose of recalling three of us, set for Tuesday, August 15. Yes, we had to vote for our own recall election. Tresham voiced the only "no." I don't know which was harder, the waiting period from April to June while the signatures were gathered, or those long summer weeks until the election. Margaret directed all her energy to the anti-recall campaign.

On a practical level, in terms of the governing of the borough, the whole recall effort meant that for ten months, ever since the initial assembly meeting on the harbor when Don first threatened a recall, every public word I spoke and each decision the three of us made was intensified by the pressure of upcoming judgment. As Tom bluntly said, it felt like someone was holding a gun to our heads in every meeting.

It was exhausting and I cried a lot. It all left me feeling as if the love of my life had cheated on me. Haines is my favorite place in the whole world. My home. The people here are my people, or so I thought. I am the town obituary writer. I have written over four hundred of them, and because we are a small place, I have not only composed those obituaries but helped grieving families during their hardest times. I often give eulogies. I thought those relationships mattered. That people might disagree with me, but they'd be kind.

The summer dragged on. My neighbor Betty fell on the Fourth of July and broke her hip, and I accompanied her to Juneau, and then she needed me more than ever once she returned home. At the end of July, I helped my daughter JJ move to the Aleutian Islands town of Unalaska, where she'd taken a job as the elementary school principal while her husband was finishing up their commitments in Juneau. Unalaska is seventeen hundred miles from Haines, and far more remote. (They had their recall election after my visit. Was I contagious?) On the way home I was picking up a new puppy in Anchorage. I was grateful for the distance my obligations put between me and the recall, in miles and in preoccupations. I would have stayed in the Aleutians for months if JJ had asked me to, and brought my puppy back to her place. The cell service was lousy and the internet worse. It was so barren yet covered in wildflowers and berries. There were few people, and no bears at all on the trails. There was a pool and a library, too. I imagined a new life in a cottage on the windswept bay. My reaction to the recall was all flight and no fight. I wished more than anything that it were over.

But I am above all a responsible person, so I returned to Haines for the first meeting in August, which I thought might be my last since the election was the following week. The most memorable comment at the meeting came from Tom. We were discussing a recent clarification of the meaning of the word "substantive"—as

in what "substantive changes" to an ordinance under consideration would require us to hold an additional public hearing. The
proposed new verbiage explained that spelling and grammar
weren't "substantive" changes but did not define what *were*. Tom
slammed his hand on the table and shouted, "Saying that a dog is
not a cat does not adequately describe a dog."

BUT DOGS DO help. When we walked the new puppy
with our old dogs, Beth and I sometimes talked about the immi-
nent election, but we tried not to dwell on it. The puppy made that
easier. Beth still thought I should have named her Diversion, but
I called her Trixie. She would be my prize if I won the recall and
also if I didn't. One thing the recall petition taught me, or I should
say my reaction to it did, was that I had to make my own happiness
and not put so much weight on other people's opinions. (I know,
it's about time; feel free to shout "duh" now.) Chip used Trixie
as an excuse not to attend the recall candidates forum hosted by
KHNS and the *Chilkat Valley News*. While I reveal my emotions
on my face, and in my tight shoulders, nervous laughter, and lately,
unpredictable tears, Chip tucks his in close to the bone. I would
have liked him to be there. To protect me, I half-joked. He said
he was afraid he might say something he'd regret. He still had a
business to run and eight guys to keep employed.

The recall supporters had decided that I was not a friend of "the
working man." That the education I'm proud of—from Friends
Academy and Middlebury College to the master's degree I earned
in 2011 from the University of Alaska Anchorage—was a liability
rather than an asset. But this is who I am. I can't pretend to be
someone I'm not.

I reminded myself of that as I dressed for the forum, choosing to put my best self forward even if it confirmed all their fears about me. Onto my finger slid my mother's emerald ring for guidance. In went my pearl earrings for grace. Ironed khaki capris exuded my common sense and decorum, since my legs would be exposed under the table, and the black short-sleeve blouse I bought in Florence, Italy, was respectful and appropriate to the occasion. It could be warm if the room was full. The Birkenstock sandals on my feet reminded me that I can walk anywhere comfortably and confirmed for all to see that I have an artist's heart and am an old lefty. My hair is cut short, naturally gray, and is the definition of sporty. I am above all a good sport, and an endurance athlete. I wore my favorite glasses to see clearly. But around my neck there was a slightly subversive silver pendant featuring a naked old lady with a book pressed against her sagging breasts. The breasts poke out below the book cover and above her round belly. No one would see my necklace, because it was not that big and because tonight she was facing backward, mooning the room.

"Just keep your head down, my friend, and you'll be fine," Margaret said.

I told myself I had nothing to prove, nothing to lose, and nothing to gain. The sides had already been chosen. I'd weathered the worst of the gossip and slander. I didn't think that the forum would change anyone's mind about me. Teresa was too nervous to come to the Chilkat Center but coached me "not to rock the boat" or give the recall any more ammunition. She promised to pray for me.

I'd written down a few points I wanted to make, beginning with a thank you to everyone who had reached out to me during the difficult time, and defending myself in a sentence or two. That was it. I had briefly practiced politely answering imagined charges against myself in the bathroom mirror. I rehearsed saying, "No thank you, I have nothing more to add."

AT THE CHILKAT Center, there was a long folding table on the stage with microphones on it and six bottles of water and six chairs. Half for "us" and half for "them." The audience filed in. Tom and Tresham arrived. Big Don, too. My hands were sweating. I twisted my mother's ring and breathed deeply. The three of us took our seats and waited for the recall proponents to take theirs. And then came an announcement from Emily, the news director from the sponsoring radio station: the recall petitioners had chosen not to participate in the forum. When they backed out, Emily and Kyle had called more than thirty other known recall supporters to represent their side this evening, but they all refused to speak. Now Emily invited anyone in the room who wanted to explain the reasons for the recall to take one of the seats next to us. No one moved, not even Big Don. Asked why he wouldn't defend his own recall, he remained seated in the audience and said, "No comment."

For months I had been attacked, lied about, made myself sick because of Don and his charges, and he was refusing to explain himself? And none of those others would, either? Were you kidding me? Where was Ryan and his truck now?

When I was asked to give my opening statement, I was shaking. So I took another long breath and stuck to my script by thanking supporters, and then dampening down the mixed emotions I felt, read from the card I'd composed at home. "The charges are baseless. I never coerced the police chief into putting the blotter back in the paper for financial gain, and receiving an email is not conducting the public's business in private, nor was that email copied to other assembly members, or part of a group email. I'm not sure how it was even determined that could be grounds for recall."

I paused. This was all I intended to say. Then I thought of Chip, and our children and friends, and of myself, to be honest. I had been wronged. If I don't stick up for myself, who will?

"In many ways, for me, the damage has been done, regardless of how the recall election ends. I have spent nearly thirty-five years here raising a family, contributing to the community in meaningful and significant ways. Whenever anybody asks me about Haines, I say, 'I love the place but it's the people more,' and that is still true, but at this point I'm feeling as if I've lost something dear. I am an obituary writer, and it feels as if there has been a death in my family, and the grief is going to stay with me. Of course, I know from my work as well that you need to love the living and continue on and that in some ways makes life sweeter, but the hurt doesn't go away, and it's not going to."

My voice caught, but I plowed on. It was my turn and I surprised myself by now intending to make every word count. In public. On the radio. "I think if we can get past this, we can do a lot of good for Haines and hopefully learn from what has happened not to behave this way again. Otherwise who will take a chance at public service?"

When Kyle and Emily asked me about the charges on the recall ballot, I said, "It strikes me as strange that a grandmother of six has somehow brought the Haines PD to its knees over the police blotter." I also confessed to everyone in town who might have thought I made a lot of money at the newspaper (and could possibly profit from having the police blotter in there!) that I am only paid $75 per obituary and they take about three days to complete. I added that Tom was not a wealthy man, nor a particularly generous employer, and everyone laughed. Tom hooted that I was making him look bad, and for the first time in months, everything felt so normal. It was as if the channel had been changed and we were now at a picnic in my backyard, and my old friends Tom and Tresham were there, and we were sitting on a log by the river and not in a hinged seat over a dunk tank at a witch trial.

The last edition of Kyle's newspaper before the election devoted half of the front page to a photo of the three of us at the long table next to the three empty seats under the headline "Recall Proponents Absent from Public Forum."

I RECEIVED MY ballot on August 15, along with everyone else who showed up at the rural polling place twenty-six miles from town, the Mosquito Lake area fire hall, or at the one in town, where the majority of Haines Borough residents vote. I wished I'd written my ballot statement as well as Tom and Tresham had. I had come very close to leaving that space blank because I was so upset. Last time the town voting place had been the Chilkat Center; this time it was the Alaska Native Brotherhood Hall, right across the street from a church and the health clinic, which I took as a positive sign. I could use all the prayers I could get, and if I passed out a doctor was near. My people, my town, would decide my fitness to serve out the remaining two years and two months of my term. My heart beat like popping corn as I read every word on the ballot, and then steadied my hand and marked "No" firmly, three times.

I fed my completed ballot into the box, and went home to walk the dogs, have dinner with Chip, and wait for the results. Once again, I listened to the radio, as I had ten months earlier. Back then I had been so full of anticipation and hope. At the recall forum I felt I'd turned a corner. I had wanted to show everyone how brave I was, and that I wouldn't back down. Kyle's headline had lifted my spirits, but now I was filled with dread and doubt and wished I'd quit instead. Big Don can have this town, I thought. I wanted to move. Unalaska here I come. Imagine hiking and biking with no fear of predators.

WHEN I HEARD the announcement that the recall had been soundly defeated, my shoulders relaxed. My head rose. I cried. Maybe it had been worth standing my ground for. Six hundred and forty-four people voted to keep me in office. That was a hundred and fifty more than voted for me the first time. The better news was that our friends and neighbors had chosen to reject the recall premise and method, and retained all three of us by about a 60 percent margin. The turnout was impressive. It would be hard to argue, as Don had in the last election, that the "right" people hadn't cast ballots. He made sure they did this time, with an urgent last-minute post-office-box-holder mailing full of reasons to vote us out.

There were no parties or parades, but the mountains looked taller and the inlet had a sparkle to it I hadn't noticed in a while. People waved and smiled at me again. My hands quit shaking so much. I slept soundly. There was another assembly meeting to prepare for, with a full agenda, so I didn't have time to figure out what it had all meant, and perhaps I never will.

Margaret, because she ran the anti-recall campaign, and Big Don, because he ran the recall, issued a brief joint statement. "We were on different sides of this issue. We may not agree but we still respect each other and our opinions. We hope all of us can do the same as we move on." There were interviews with the local and statewide press in which the divisive politics of the times and social media were blamed, and Haines was lauded for not tipping to the dark side in dark times. But still I couldn't help myself from thinking now and again about the 415 voters who believed I was lying and incompetent.

"Not necessarily," Chip said as we sat on the porch before dinner with Pearl and the puppy. Trixie was chewing everything, as Chip had anticipated. He had not been keen on another dog. "We'll never be able to go to Paris," he had said. As if that had ever been the plan for our upcoming fortieth wedding anniversary. Now Chip picked her up off his shoe, prying the wet laces gently from her little teeth, plopped her in his lap, and offered her a piece of cheese. He handed another one to Pearl, who is more his dog than mine, and as usual was behaving perfectly. "Those people never voted for you and never will. That's life," he said.

Chip's right. The only difference between the recall election and my first election was that this time the people who voted against me had names. I also knew that if they felt that I had not done a good job of representing them, it meant that I hadn't. That was true. On the other hand, there were only so many hours in my day. When I was elected, I had assumed that people would come to meetings, read the paper, call or email or stop me on the sidewalk if they had concerns, that they would let me know. I don't spend my nights in the bars or mornings in the coffee shops. When I'm not writing, I take a hike or a bike ride or babysit grandchildren or visit Betty. So I had not picked up on how much animosity there was toward the new tilt to the left in local politics at a time when the nation and the state had swung further right.

My biggest regret was how much the recall had affected Chip. "Are you okay?" I asked him.

"Yes. I'm fine," he said. "I'm particularly pleased that none of the three of you were recalled. That's good news for our town."

So maybe this was still our town.

Democracy is not a winner-takes-all institution. It's a partnership based on the "suspicion," as E. B. White wrote, in an interesting twist on the word that is usually synonymous with doubt and lack of trust, that a little more than half of the people are right a little more than half of the time. The night before the recall election, my friend Annie gave me a copy of Yeats's poem "The Lake Isle of Innisfree." She highlighted, "And I shall have some peace there, for peace comes dropping slow." So does reconciliation in any broken relationship. It takes unlikely routes. Betty has moved to Haines Assisted Living. Her three regular visitors are Big Don, his wife, and me. So far, we haven't met in the hallway coming or going, but Betty has shared some of Don's smoked salmon with me. It's good.

‖‖‖

Manager and Committee Reports

Children's Librarian Holly Davis is back from the national
Collaborative Summer Library Program's annual summit, where
she shared ideas with librarians from all over the United States,
Guam, American Samoa, and Micronesia.

The combined Senior Center and Chilkat Valley Preschool project is
moving forward. They have started to lay the foundation and should be
framing the addition soon.

The water tests for twenty residences of concern revealed no issues with
lead or copper contamination.

The new heating unit has been installed in the pool, making the water
a consistent 81 degrees.

Parks & Rec is moving forward with the bicycle-friendly community
application and discussed concerns about bears and humans in the
Chilkoot River corridor.

‖‖‖

TWELVE

Be Like Ray

MY HUSBAND AND I are sitting by the warm woodstove. Chip shares apples and cheese with our two golden retrievers drooling on the arm of his easy chair and fast-forwards to our favorite segment of the *PBS NewsHour*: the week in review with *New York Times* columnist David Brooks and nationally syndicated columnist Mark Shields. Shields is a slightly scrappy and quick-witted old-school Democrat from Massachusetts and Brooks is an urbane intellectual moderate conservative who favors Republican values, or what they used to be, he's opined lately. When Gail Collins was editor of the *Times* opinion page, she chose Brooks to replace longtime conservative pundit William Safire because, she said, she needed to find a conservative who was likable enough to keep *Times* readers from throwing the paper out the window. Afterward, Brooks noted that while that may have been the case, he had never been so hated in his life as he was by *Times* liberals that first year. It shocked him. Imagine how he must feel these days when the country is so polarized that columnists are reviled by people who don't even read what they write, just because they believe the entire press is somehow the enemy. Heck, we think we know who is with us or against us by the cars we drive and the foods we eat.

You know us—Chip and me—too. We are stereotypical in a lot of ways: husband, wife, golden retrievers, an old Oriental rug on the floor and lots of books on the shelves, watching PBS and sipping cabernet and a local IPA. And yet. Chip is a registered Republican, there's moose stew in the crock-pot (we shot it and butchered it), and an icon of Mary and baby Jesus rests on the mantel below the wide moose antlers. I have been a Democrat since I was eighteen. Although Chip and I are in different parties, we do see eye to eye on most politics and usually vote the same way. He has become more of a Democrat thanks to the Obamas, whom he admires very much on many levels. Chip's a jazz fan and reads widely, too. Trump's rise to power sent him diving further in my direction. If Chip dropped his party affiliation, we'd prob- ably receive fewer robo-calls. But it is fun to answer the red- or blue-funded surveys in unexpected ways. And I think Chip is still hoping that the party of Lincoln will rise from the ashes. He is conservative in habits, speech, spending, and business, yet liberal when it comes to social issues—he could not care less who marries whom or whether a person identifies as he, she, or they, as long as they don't harm others. We are regular churchgoers and try to see the world with Gospel eyes, as one bishop advised. Chip has a safe full of hunting rifles and makes his own bullets but would never join the NRA because he supports gun control. He also believes people like us, who have a lot, should support programs and institutions for those who don't. I guess you could say he's an old-fashioned, decent man. Which is why I love him.

We both enjoy watching and listening to Brooks and Shields spar about the week's events from opposite sides of the political spectrum while remaining friendly.

"I want us to be like them when I grow up," I tell Chip. By "us" I mean Haines.

"Too late," Chip says.

"No, it's not. I'm a lifelong learner."

For as long as I can remember the Haines School District's mission statement has included a line about graduating "lifelong learners," a term championed by Ray Menaker. Beginning in 1974, Ray served on what was then the combined school board and borough assembly for twenty-four years.

Tonight, as usual, Brooks and Shields disagree on some fundamental points but are not completely at odds. Both bemoan the new lows to which American politics and political discourse have sunk, and both condemn Trump's leadership, pointing to the example he's setting by disgracing the institution of the presidency and even worse, encouraging a new type of leader, one less concerned about problem-solving and more bent on trampling over others to get what his or her supporters want. Mark Shields blames it on human nature, saying, "Politics is the most imitative of all human activities."

If that's true, then whom do I imitate? I will never be as solidly calm as Stephanie. Margaret was my first role model, but then she resigned from the assembly. Mike seemed to have a good head and heart for politics, but then he quit, too. Granted, he said it was because we hired Debra for borough manager instead of his favorite, Brad, but Mike was also the man who said that once a decision is made the assembly needs to stand by it even if as individuals we object. I think Mike's early exit had to do with his health. He was already in his eighties and had served several terms in office by then, and he was tired. The assembly has no two-term members right now.

How did Ray Menaker survive eight terms? That seems like a lifetime. It could not have been easy, since for starters he was a self-described Socialist. He was also from New York, a Columbia grad, and taught high school French and journalism after settling in Haines with his wife and young family in 1955, in what was then a logging and sawmill town. Ray was a WWII navy veteran and a pacifist who withheld his income tax during the Vietnam War and traveled to the Soviet Union during the Cold War. He wrote regular letters of advice and dissent to every president from Eisenhower onward.

Inspired by the student newspaper, Ray and one of his students decided to start a community weekly, which became the *Chilkat Valley News*. They printed it themselves, typesetting pages with those old metal letters on an old-fashioned press. Ray was a founder of our public radio station, too, served on its board, and produced a weekly KHNS program called "Tales and Tunes," reading stories from his favorite authors—from James Thurber and Saki to O. Henry and Shakespeare—and played music from the likes of Paul Robeson, Édith Piaf, and Pete Seeger. He was a founding member of Lynn Canal Conservation, an environmental group that helped create the forty-thousand-acre Chilkat Bald Eagle Preserve in Haines, and with his wife, Vivian, was a strong advocate of early childhood education. Vivian, with Ray's support, started the first preschool in Haines. Ray loved acting and theater, performing in or directing a play or two every year. For decades he was Lynn Canal Community Players' treasurer, the position in any organization that often takes the most work.

Ray performed a rope trick in Chilkat Center variety shows. He'd walk on the stage with a coiled line and announce that he could throw one end up in the air and it would stay up there by force of will. He spoke very seriously, lecturing the audience that we must all concentrate completely as well, and believe with our whole hearts that he could actually do this. When he felt everyone understood their role in the success of his trick, i.e., the power of positive thinking, he'd slowly wind up, and with much antic-ipation, fling the rope into the air. After it fell back to the floor, he would pivot, point a finger at an audience member and yell, "There's a skeptic in the house!"

I WROTE AND delivered Ray's eulogy. As I was working on it, Tom, who by then had become the publisher of the *Chilkat Valley News*, wanted to make sure I noted that Ray was "very much the counterpoint" to John Schnabel, Debra and Roger's father— you'll remember that Debra is now the borough manager and Roger hauled those rocks through the hillside neighborhood. John owned the sawmills and several other businesses, from a hardware store to a motel, and was our town's first, and maybe only, captain of industry. While John was building up Main Street and his for-tune, Ray was pumping his resources, mostly human, into cultural and social institutions that have remained long after John's mills closed.

That former student of Ray's who had started the paper with him told me that when he looks back on all the criticism Ray received as the paper's editor and as an assembly member, he is amazed by how even-tempered and easy-going he was. Bill said, "I never heard him say anything negative about anyone, though he was puzzled by people and their attitudes sometimes." Bill said that when Ray was accused of being a card-carrying Communist and dubbed "Red Ray" during the McCarthy era, it was seriously disconcerting, so he went right to the source of the rumor and spent an hour explaining the distinctions between socialism, communism, and capitalism.

ON THE *PBS NewsHour* when David Brooks observed that "you can be depressed" about national politics if you choose, but the good news is that "on the state and city level politics is working pretty good," I snorted my wine out my nose.

"It's all roses out here in the provinces," I said, wiping my face.

I can't say for certain if the level of ill will, distrust, and plain meanness I experienced in my term was inspired by the president's Tweets and lies, as Brooks and Shields surmised, or if it was simply a lot more of the same old societal pressure to feel the safety, security, and comfort of belonging that is as ancient as the tribes of Israel.

I believe that Trump's rhetoric both empowers and frightens people. At the time of the recall I wondered if national politics floated up to small-town Alaska. Now I'm wondering if Haines politics drifted south. It's probably some of both, with social media grabbing the helm during the stormiest moments.

Our recall election was not the first in Haines, and probably won't be the last. Ray, with all his years in office mostly behind him by then, was even a subject of a 1993 recall election over an executive session, or private meeting, about a personnel issue involving a principal's contract. In this case, the superintendent wanted the principal fired. The school board, which at the time was also the assembly, emerged from behind the closed door and voted 5–1 to keep her. A group of people, some of them parents of students but not all, objected in large part to keeping the principal because she had new ideas about education, which included learning the local Native ways, and favored other methods of assessing student progress besides standard grades and report cards. She also liked yoga and lived out on Mud Bay Road. In other words, she was one of "those" people, and not one of "theirs."

Ray won his recall election, but two other assembly/school board members didn't, and a third quit rather than suffer the weeks of scandal prior to the vote. There were so many hard feelings over the injustice of it all that a self-taught local legal expert (who was not an attorney) managed to take the argument against the propriety of that recall election all the way to the Alaska Supreme Court and win. It took over a year to resolve, however, and by then the damage had been done and new assembly/school board members were in place. The court's decision to overturn the election results was moot, although the judge ordered the group who sponsored the recall, the Committee for an Honest and Ethical School Board, to pay the $20,000 or so in borough attorney fees. A committee member responded to a Haines reporter's request for a comment on the ruling with: "Who is the Supreme Court? They don't live here."

Ray never took criticism personally and he never avoided confrontations. What was most important to him was making sure every voice was heard and that all views were at least considered. He asked a lot of questions in an attempt to learn more about the issues and equally important, why people with differing viewpoints held them. He was curious at his core, and pleasant to speak with, always. He was never in a hurry and he didn't argue. He listened.

If *NewsHour*'s Judy Woodruff ever interviews me, I only hope I'm half as wise as Ray was and calmly deem my recall experience the likely result of tribal politics in fearful and divisive times. Maybe. Maybe I'd sum it up by saying that a group of conservative, anti-intellectual men, mostly, influenced by right-wing pundits and President Trump's combative, winner-takes-all politics, encouraged by their friends at the bars, coffee shops, and miners' association meetings, saw my progressive values—protecting the environment; funding the arts center, museum, and library; letting kids swim for free at the pool; helping to ensure the school has a band, choir, and art class; lowering speed limits and promoting bike lanes; questioning the authority of police, the mayor, the manager, the harbor officials, and anyone in power; improving the town's appearance with landscaping and paint—as a threat to theirs. They were upset that I, and my spiritual kinsmen Tom and Tresham, had been elected and they used state law to try to un-elect us. I guess I'm still a tad angry. I know, I need to move on. As Brooks and Shields, and I suspect Ray would say, it was much ado about nothing. Change may come, as it usually does, in the next general election.

And maybe, in spite of the big-picture differences, Brooks has a point about local governments. These days, with the recall behind us, the assembly is working together better than the US Congress is, mainly because we have to—there is a lot to do to keep a town functioning. Budgets, contracts, Code revisions, tour permits. Old trucks have to be repaired or sold, sewer pumps need to work, trail plans need to be approved, and the freight dock has to be replaced. This also explains why, even if Ray was a Socialist and an environmentalist, he was reelected so many times: he was knowledgeable, fair, and thrifty when it came to everyday matters.

Still, I often feel like certain assembly members and I speak such entirely different languages that we might as well be from different countries. During a bathroom break at a recent meeting Assemblywoman Brenda Josephson explained to me that she believed it was the assembly's job to automatically cut the manager's proposed annual budget before passing it. She said we could not raise taxes without first slashing spending.

But why, I wondered? The budget is balanced and provides for the services residents want and need and the personnel to accomplish them. And as the manager said in presenting the budget to us, the majority of residents expect us to provide the services they have come to count on. I guess these are not the people Brenda hangs out with. She chose to target two of my favorite places in town—the library and the swimming pool. I chose to be like Ray and not take her judgments personally. I reckoned that her desire to curb spending was more about the principle of tightening belts than about real necessity, because it's not as if the Haines Borough budget is fat. Volunteers fill in the gaps left by staff so the library can be open evenings and weekends. Volunteers also water the plants in the pool atrium and chaperone swimming lessons. Lifeguards earn about fourteen dollars an hour.

"Times are hard. I'm worried," Brenda said in the women's room, echoing Alaska's current conservative governor. Brenda was afraid of the consequences of continuing Alaska's entitled ways. She felt that taxes should fund *only* essential services and needs. This place is tiny. I didn't argue. Instead, from the other side of the stall I reminded her that libraries are even more critical in economic downturns, because they offer free access to information technology and educational material, keep children safe after school or during evenings when parents are working, and provide a warm, comfortable place for community members to gather and feel welcome in a space that belongs to all of us. They also offer lots to read, I said. "The reason the library deserves all the funding we can give it," I continued, "is that it is the only taxpayer-funded facility, department, or organization that is available to every single resident from infants to elders, seven days a week year-round. The school isn't, the harbor isn't."

She didn't respond.

As we washed our hands, though, Brenda smiled and said that she couldn't disagree more. She said she planned to introduce the budget amendments anyway, at the next meeting, to continue the debate in public.

There was no shouting, and as far I detected, no animosity. We were not exactly PBS commentators, but we were not screaming at each other. This wasn't MSNBC or Fox News, either. Were we *both* being like Ray?

As we walked back down the hall before the recess was over, Brenda asked me to consider her proposal for dropping the assembly stipend to just twenty-five dollars for each regular meeting, or from thirty-five hundred dollars a year to about six hundred. Why not show good faith in trimming the expenses and cut our paychecks? I told her I would love to support her, and as far I am concerned, personally, would agree, but that as a responsible assembly member, I can't. I knew that something similar had once been contemplated by assembly/school board members following a decline in student enrollment and state budget cuts that caused teachers to be laid off. Back then liberal Ray, with his gray beard and homespun woolen socks tucked into well-worn Birkenstocks, objected, even though everyone knew that he gave away all his checks to the preschool.

Ray explained that nothing prevented the school board members from donating their money to the art class or the school band, but a meaningful stipend must remain policy in case someone needed it to pay for gas to drive to meetings, babysitters, increased phone bills, or the cost of paper and pens. Some people could afford to do without the check. Others now and in the future may not, and for that reason eliminating it was wrong.

Since Brenda and I were already back in our adjacent seats at the dais, I couldn't share all that history with her. "You and I don't need the money," I told her—she's an executive with the largest construction company in town; we have relative affluence in common—"but someone else might." The assembly is already elite enough, with retirees and those of us with flexible schedules in the majority. Given the time demands of governing, we shouldn't make it any more difficult to hold local office than it already is.

ALL OF THE organizations Ray helped found and championed are still thriving, some more than fifty years later. Which is a long time in a place that only became a state sixty years ago. Ray had a "Question Authority" bumper sticker on his car. That could have been the mission statement for his paper, which Kyle now owns and runs. Ray died before Kyle came to town, but it is kind of weird and wonderful that in Kyle's office there is a new sign that reads, "Asking questions is not being negative." Ray did not push his broader political agenda onto local boards or government. Instead, he encouraged people to think about and research the consequences of their choices and make sure they were informed ones. As a teacher, Ray knew that you can't make someone change his or her mind—they have to do that on their own.

Ray lived a long and, by all accounts, happy life, both in and out of thousands of meetings, when he died peacefully in 2015 at Haines Assisted Living at age 93. The assisted living administrator, who was also a Catholic deacon and an old friend of Ray's said, "We're all supposed to think globally, but Ray's life showed what a person can do locally. You think of what he did for this little slice of the earth. He was focused on his hometown."

One postscript: All his life, Ray Menaker challenged John Schnabel over logging practices. Ray fought to block John from clear-cutting local forests. The stories from that era say mill hands slashed greenies' tires. Well, it would turn out that John and Ray spent the last years of their lives sharing meals and sitting in recliners by the fire at Haines Assisted Living. They behaved like perfect gentlemen toward each other. On the other hand, they were both stone deaf by then and couldn't actually listen to each other even if they'd chosen to.

Manager and Committee Reports:

The harbor staff reports that after beaching the Letnikof Cove Harbor float they discovered some damage, but it should be repairable.

The Public Safety Commission meeting on drug abuse issues was well attended, informative, and directive. Attendees recognized that enforcement is not a solution, though generally supported greater financial support for the police department.

The Finance Dept. reports that tax statements are at the printers and should be distributed next week.

Public Works has reconsidered the recommendation to dike the Klehini River to protect the Porcupine Road. Do you want to pursue the option of maintaining the Sunshine Mountain Road as an alternative route?

The construction at the wastewater treatment plant is ahead of schedule.

THIRTEEN

Looking in a Broken Mirror

RUMI WROTE THAT the truth was a mirror that God dropped and all we have left to guide us are the little pieces of it we have picked up. No one knows the whole truth of anything, no matter what we swear to in court with our hand lightly on that Bible. Still, we have to keep looking for it in order to arrive at the best outcome we can. This may seem like a roundabout way of getting to one true story of our town that changed us, but bear with me. This is a story of crime and cover-up, of individual guilt and also collective responsibility. And that is why it is also a tale about government.

Friends broke the news of her husband's death by suicide to Haines's beloved school principal René Martin while she was on the ferry returning home from a regional school event with students, parents, and teachers. It was awful, tragic, and sad. The school community was shaken and did their best to support her, as did so many others. Residents began to talk more openly than we ever had before about suicide, partly to process this death and partly to prevent more such deaths. Rick Martin had been a janitor at the school, and he was a gentle, kind man who was known to all the kids. Lately, he had become the primary caregiver for his sick, elderly mother, moving her into his and René's home, even though Rick was also terminally ill with organ failure. That helped explain his death. Alaskans above all are independent and understand when someone does not want to die far from home and full of tubes. (You may recall that Haines has no hospital.)

When I met with René to write Rick's obituary, I was struck by how strong and frank she was. She managed to be both Rick's wife *and* the principal, the leader of our elementary, middle, and high schools. These are all under one roof, so children of all ages, from my kindergartener granddaughters to the high school seniors, walk in the same double doors every morning and exit each afternoon. The largest chunk of the borough budget goes to the school. The joint annual meeting between the assembly and the school board is one of mutual admiration and cooperation. It is by far the most pleasant meeting of the year and takes place in the bright, well-used school library.

When René spoke to me about Rick at her kitchen table, there were tears, but they were tempered with concern for her students. Rick had grown up in Haines and during the big timber years he worked as a logger and equipment operator in a camp located on an island in southeast Alaska. He was a great high school athlete and had been a star on the Haines adult basketball team as a young man. Lately, Chip and I had seen him most summer mornings when we rode bikes. He'd be cruising the same roads we were in his blue pickup with a yellow dog riding shotgun. There are not a lot of people up and out the door before 7:00 a.m. Sometimes we'd see Rick three times in a thirty-mile ride as we all doubled back on different scenic loops of town. He no doubt appreciated the views, too, and was taking a read on the news of nature, looking for the first whales in the inlet, bears on the Chilkoot River, moose in the meadow at the bend in the road by the airport. Rick slowed and waved when he passed us. A man in his element, content and, like us, habitual. I enjoyed his company, which is what it felt like even though we didn't speak. I'm shy of traffic, but I felt safe around Rick and that happy dog, as if they were watching out for us.

Rick loved dogs, his and everyone else's. Above all, he loved René. She had been working at Christy Fowler's Pioneer Bar and Bamboo Room Restaurant for years when, in middle age, she decided to become a teacher. She enrolled as a full-time undergrad at the University of Alaska, moved up to Fairbanks, and lived near campus. Rick found work up there to be with her. "He believed in me. He made change possible," René said. After teaching high school English here, she earned her administrative degree and was made our principal.

On March 11, before ending his life, Rick videotaped a message for his loved ones. René felt it was important that people hear directly from her about Rick's death and her response to it, so she let me know what he had said in the recording. "He told us he loved us. He was proud of us, and he was so, so sorry but he was in too much pain." She also wanted everyone to know that her husband lamented the current divisiveness and negativity, nationally and locally. "Rick really wanted us to be kind, to be positive, to be good to one another," she said. Finally, she wanted to make sure that others who were feeling depressed would not be moved to copy Rick. "His choice is not for us. There are many people who care, that love you, and that want to help you. Please ask," she said, and I wrote.

Kyle called late on deadline night and asked if he could run the headline for the obituary by me. I rarely get input on them—that's the editor's prerogative. "How's this?" he said. "Martin's Last Wish a Plea for Community Kindness."

I told him it was perfect. That was the Rick I knew.

A FEW DAYS later, we found out that Rick had left another message for René, one that initially she had not revealed. He said he had been raped as a student by Karl Ward, who had taught and coached at the school, and eventually became the Haines Borough School District superintendent in the last years of his twenty-two-year career there before retiring in 1976. Karl was a legend by the time I arrived in Haines in 1984. All superintendents were measured against his tenure. Karl hadn't just sat in the district office and done paperwork. He knew all the kids by name. The Karl Ward Gymnasium was home to the Glacier Bears high school basketball, volleyball, wrestling, and cheer teams, and the men's and women's adult league teams. The gymnasium is our town's athletic and recreation center and, along with the library just across the school fields from it, is the beating heart of our community.

Rick had made some comments to René over the years about his dislike of Karl, as had others who apparently knew him well, but René had not realized the extent of his anger or the why of it until his posthumous message. Before René went to the radio and the newspaper with her news—which she would ultimately do—she or perhaps her friends removed the big name plaque in the gym. René didn't need to wait to go through proper channels, whatever they may have been in this case, because Karl could not object. He had died in 1997. She did it for Rick, and for the others she believed were among us.

Over twenty years ago, right after Karl Ward died, I had asked his grieving wife, Doris, who was as stricken as René was now, if there was anything I could do for her. She asked me to take over the social column she wrote in the *Chilkat Valley News*. It was called "Duly Noted" and it kept track of all the local comings and goings, weddings and graduations, with names in bold. It was nothing earth-shattering, really, but I still can hear Doris telling me, "Nothing you ever write will be as important as the stories of the people in this town." From that vote of confidence and with that admonition I went on to compose obituaries, write national columns, and publish books.

I had only known Karl as Doris's husband, a well-respected, ill, older man. He made the graduating senior male athletes scrapbooks with newspaper clippings and photographs and mementos from their high school years playing basketball or running cross-country and track. They were treasured by the seniors I coached on the cross-country team. Everything I knew about Karl Ward was honorable and generous. Truth is, I didn't know him any better than I really knew Rick. Doris is now past ninety and resides in Haines Assisted Living. She likes me to bring her pretty pebbles back from my bike rides for her collection. I remain torn as I write this now because it will cause her pain, and I adore her. But God help us, look what our town's collective silence did to Rick. If someone had intervened sooner would he have been spared his assaults?

KHNS OFFICIALLY BROKE the news. Abbey Collins, a crackerjack young reporter, worked with some seasoned colleagues to craft the shocking but accurate story. At their best, news organizations bring communities closer together by presenting all the facts, or as many as possible, without judgment. This is what people crave in difficult times. The free press asks our questions for us and investigates them in a way that allows emotional stories to be processed individually—and ultimately, one hopes, collectively.

I listened to the first story about Rick and Karl on the radio while standing alone in my kitchen. Debra, the borough manager, was being interviewed. She said she believed René and Rick. Debra told KHNS that when she was growing up in Haines many people had "suspicions" about Karl Ward and she'd heard hushed stories that, over time, she came to believe "must be true, because there was so much of it." She was also certain there were others besides Rick. "This is one person's story," she said speaking to listeners directly. "And if it's happened to you, then it's our story. I know as the manager of this borough, it's our story as a community." She explained that her reason for coming forward now about the rumors she'd heard then was that, like René, she wanted to bring Haines's dark past to light so that nobody else would suffer as Rick had.

Unlike Debra, there were plenty of people in town who said they'd heard nothing about this at the time. Some denied the story completely. After all, it was hard to take in. When I was in college a history professor cautioned us students not to believe everything we read about the past or assumed to be true based on our own biases: our education to date, our family of origin, our mentors. He said the devil does not always appear with horns and a red cape. The most dangerous people were often the ones who look and act like us and were part of our family or group.

Now I'm thinking of the seemingly sweet old man down on the basketball court sitting in a wheelchair and smiling as the boys on the team all circled around him and rubbed his bald head for good luck before the tip-off. He had also been a Boy Scout leader; a Presbyterian missionary who taught at the old Haines House home for Native children; a foster parent before he and Doris were married; and of course a coach—he'd received all kinds of accolades over the years, locally, regionally and statewide, for his close relationships with students, especially basketball-playing boys.

Haines is fortunate to have both a public radio station with daily newscasts and a weekly newspaper that covers local news in more depth. Statewide public media did not pick up the radio story at first, supposedly because both the accuser and the accused were dead and so there was no way to prove its truth, they said. At the *Chilkat Valley News*, though, Kyle never hesitated. After the radio story, he spent the days before his weekly paper came out learning more, asking tough questions, and confirming stories and the reliability of sources.

When the hints of doubt from outside news outlets filtered through Haines and into the quiet conversations in coffee shops, pillow whispers between a wife and her husband late at night, or maybe even in a look shared by two former teammates of Rick's across the bar, other victims decided it was time to speak. Remember at that time, the president was denigrating the press, shouting about fake news. Remember, too, that Haines's local recall supporters had made their own news on Facebook, preferring it to traditional media. They even used our newspaper connection against Tom and me.

Kyle was the new kid on the block. He did not have a history with the community or the individuals he was reporting on. At the same time, he had just invested everything he had in a business here, the paper. Maybe that's part of the reason Karl Ward's other victims spoke to Kyle. He was taking a risk, too. Or maybe it was because he would not judge them against the past. It was time, finally, to put the pieces of the mirror together.

That week, I bought the paper as soon as a bundle of them were dropped in the rack at the grocery store. I couldn't wait until the one I'd already paid for by subscription was folded into my mailbox at the post office a few hours later. I read it sitting in my car on Main Street. The people parked in front of me and behind me were doing the same thing. Others leaned on doorframes with the paper open and, later, sat silently reading at tables at Mountain Market, standing in the post office, or behind a closed door at work while their voice mail took a message.

Kyle had interviewed former teachers and students. He spoke with René. He heard and maybe saw Rick's video, since he quoted it. Rick had told the truth. And Craig Loomis was the first to con-firm it. Craig? Had I read that right? Our Craig? Who lent my son his first deer hunting rifle and taught him how to spit off a dock like "a real man" when he was ten, and who had made major messes of my stove frying up deer and moose meat. Who was always clown-ing around while carrying his own grief all these years?

I kept reading.

Craig was a sixteen-year-old basketball player when he was fondled by Karl Ward while he was at the Wards' house drink-ing with the other players. Underage drinking at a schoolteacher's house? How could that ever have happened? "For these people to sit there and tell the public that's now in Haines that they never knew anything, I call BS. They heard about it." Sorry would be a start, Craig went on to say. That sounded like the Craig I knew.

In his video, Rick had said that after he told his father what happened, his father replied that there was nothing they could do, as they were Native and powerless against the most powerful man in town. He told Rick to stay away from Karl Ward. Craig, who is not Native, wondered out loud if his life would have been different had he trusted teachers and done better in school and gone to college. He has had a good life, though, he said, with a long, happy marriage, two kids he's close to, and now the joy of grandchildren. Craig went to counseling after the intensity of the story died down some and reached out to other victims who did not want to go public to talk with them. Mostly, he said, he feels guilty for not speaking up sooner, for not stopping what had happened to Rick and, he knows, others. At the time, he didn't realize he wasn't the only one.

The healing, which I know sounds trite, but was genuine, began as soon as that plaque was removed, either by the principal or with her blessing. Karl's victims would be believed. This time the people in charge of our community were on their side. Debra, the borough manager, had spoken. The school board made a heartfelt and appropriate statement, noting that these crimes happened decades ago and that policies and procedures were in place to do all in the district's power to prevent such abuse from happening again. We all had to be on guard for our children, though. Their well-being was up to all of us. Craig and three other men had told their stories. The police chief had told the paper that Karl's crimes followed a pattern he'd seen before in other communities. "He brings in kids that are already torn out of their home that really have no voice . . . He was probably given a certain level of trust when he came in with the Presbyterian Mission and the Haines

House and he goes into the public school system, and that level of trust just continued. He operated in the shadows based on that level of trust."

BUT WHAT ABOUT what Craig had said? About leaders who did nothing while this was happening? I am part of that leadership now. Mayor Jan Hill was a student at the school when Karl Ward worked there. She should speak for us. The mayor is fairly stoic, but she became emotional telling me a story about a young man she knew—he was basically family, Jan said—who had been a good ball player, a nice kid, who drifted into trouble and alcohol, and one day left town. She teared up when she said no one knew what had happened to him. Now she thought she did. This might be our town's history we were airing, but for Jan, it was personal.

I volunteered to help write a statement from the assembly that the mayor would deliver. Jan and I had always been on opposite ends of the political spectrum, and we often disagreed on specific issues. We still do. But today we also share what I believe is a mutual respect—and this helped us. Back then, Jan was not sure about accepting my offer. I explained that I had written speeches for Stephanie when she was mayor, and that I had helped many people compose their eulogies. It took a few days. We talked some more and worked on the final draft. At the beginning of the next assembly meeting, her voice steady, Jan read: "In the matter of the late school superintendent of schools, Karl Ward, our community collectively failed to meet this most sacred responsibility, resulting in harm to a generation of our students. While we cannot undo the injury suffered by the victims, we offer to them our most sincere apology, and humbly ask for their forgiveness."

She promised that what happened in the past would never be repeated and stressed that our school was a safe place, and so was Haines by nearly all standards. However, she said, sexual assault and alcohol-related crimes do happen, and too often are ignored or downplayed by residents who choose to look the other way. She called for light to shine on our problems in order to cure them.

Though I had helped craft the words, Jan spoke with a deeper knowledge about the present pain and the past wrongs and denials than I had ever known, as well as of a future where "physical and emotional aggression of any kind, from anyone, especially from those of us who yield authority or power over others, will not be tolerated." She said that the time had come to encourage conversations that we may have avoided in the past. "If something seems off to you, with a friend, a neighbor, a situation, ask hard questions, listen honestly to the answers. Offer assistance. All of us must work together to give a voice to the voiceless and be a witness to the good at the heart of this caring community."

I had feared Rick's story would literally tear the town apart. That didn't happen. If anything, a kind of calm settled over Haines in the days and weeks after the news broke. We agreed not to disagree on accepting our collective guilt, about apologizing, about doing everything in our power to make sure it never was repeated. There was relief that the secret was finally out. There was no alternative news challenging the victims' stories or René's actions on their behalf. When the statewide and then the national news did pick up the story, it was more for the sensationalism of the revelations, unfortunately, than the efficacy of the local response.

There would be no trial, no dramatic moment when the victims and their families faced the abuser—he was long gone. The men who had been victims did not want to say more about it publicly, but Craig and the counseling services were quietly helping not only Karl's victims but others who now felt they too could speak without shame of their past.

Revelations like Rick's, actions like René's and Craig's, and the rest who stepped forward, as well as reporting like Kyle's and the unified statements from leaders on the school board, in the borough, in law enforcement, and social workers mattered. There was some talk immediately following the news about forming a local Truth and Reconciliation Commission, similar to the ones in our nearest neighbor, Canada, to address the past crimes and abuses in public institutions, schools, and communities committed against children, especially Native children, and their families by missionaries and teachers. Perhaps some of Craig's conversations will lead to one here. Perhaps a new generation of leaders will press the issue of reparations and accountability. I'm certain that at some point more hard truths will be revealed. I only hope it does not take forty more years, or another death.

In the meantime, each of us needs to take care of ourselves and those we are close to, and we have to watch out for one another's backs, too. I cannot add up how many times I have responded to local gossip, which can be vicious, with "that may be true for you, but so-and-so has never been anything but nice to me," or "I'll believe that when I see it." My greatest hurdle in public office has been separating the issues from the people. I err on the side of friends when I'm stressed, because those relationships are what matter most to me personally. I have not always seen the whole mirror but merely what is reflected in the little pieces I choose to keep in my pocket. I have, as I confess every Sunday in church, left undone those things that I ought to have done, and left unsaid those things that in hindsight I ought to have said.

WHEN I PICK up my grandchildren at school, see them run toward me with backpacks and braids flapping, and René is in the hall with Rick's dog at her side, and Leigh is at the library door, and Tiana is minding the front desk, I am grateful and yes, happy, for so much love. For most of us—and this may sound like denial, but it's true—on any given week, day, or moment like this one at school, Haines is beautiful and generous, safe and friendly, perhaps even more so now that the initial violence of the storm has passed and the sun is back out. If you are wondering how that can be, well, don't you carry several versions of the truth in your heart simultaneously about the people and places you love? Don't you think everyone does? Real life, real people working out really big issues meaningfully, takes time, and patience. Haines, like all communities, is a work in progress, and the ending of this story is yet to come.

Manager and Committee Reports:

The first cruise ship of the season was May 21. It was the largest ship we will host this year and unfortunately was greeted with an unseasonable weather event that put a bit of a damper on the visit. However Tourism and Harbor staff did an excellent job of accommodating guests to ensure it was a positive experience.

The state senate has fully funded public radio, and it doesn't appear the Haines state forester position will be cut. Education has been cut, and they are asking the ferry system to generate more revenue. Tourism and seafood marketing have been funded to last year's level.

The floats at Letnikof Harbor are in for the season and the ramps there and at the Port Chilkoot Dock have been lowered.

★ FOURTEEN ★

Nature Remains

THE LIGHT IS back, more than twelve hours out of twenty-four, and we are gaining five minutes a day until summer solstice. If I tell you that on one of these mornings, when the tide is out and the sun is up and I am walking on the mud flats, I will sing an old spiritual about falling on my knees with my face to the rising sun, and then do it, oh Lord have mercy, will you keep that to yourself? I sometimes dance like Gene Kelly (or at least imagine I can) to my own versions of show tunes, too. Keep that under your hat as well. Some things are private. Nothing lifts me out of winter's funk more than these light mornings and evenings. There are setbacks. Nature teaches me to expect them. Spring in Alaska can behave like a tipsy date, dancing a wobbly waltz. One step forward and two steps back.

In the last week alone, there have been three winter storms. Snow, rain, wind, ice, frozen ground, and sun all conspired to flood roads and driveways, ditches and yards. As debris from the runoff from one rainstorm blocked a culvert on the road, the low place between my daughter Stoli's house and ours filled with water, and the only way to free it meant cutting a trench to the sea through the thick dam of slabs of beached ice. Most of it was a foot or more thick. I couldn't break through it completely, but I could dig a groove to channel the water. I like spring yard work, and in Alaska that often involves a shovel rather than a rake, or even a pickax, which I keep handy for just such emergencies. I swung the pick and hacked at the ice, and the water filled in behind the cut. Hack, flow, hack, flow . . . soon gallons and gallons gushed down to the sandy shore. It was impressive, if I do say so myself.

It felt so good busting up the hard, dirty ice of winter and watching the water run free that, as the water drained, I made the channel deeper. I kept at it for hours. I took off my hat and mittens, then my jacket. The drizzle ceased and the warming sun steamed up the ice and my glasses, which I tucked in my pocket for safekeeping. Sweat dripped into my eyes. Blisters popped on my palms, mud splattered, ice chips flew, and the dogs looked alarmed as I groaned and heaved and smashed that ax down, laughing like a mad woman. A sound like thunder finally stopped me. I turned around in time to witness an avalanche of rock and snow roil down a mountain. What a gift. Sometimes a woman needs to swing a pick and break up ice. Sometimes God needs to shake the weight of winter off her mountains, too. It was nice to know I wasn't alone.

The assembly has had another burst of productivity recently, as well, one that also could be attributed to the increasing daylight and the season's urgings to spend evenings outdoors rather than inside at meetings. The last agenda packet was only thirty-five pages long and our actions on it were quick and decisive. We voted unanimously to write a letter to the legislature in support of allowing the local distillery to serve cocktails in the tasting room and to promote a postcard writing campaign to demand state lawmakers fund the ferry service, since between breakdowns and storms, Haines was without timely, reliable service most of the winter. This is already a difficult place to get to and from. Ferries and small planes connect Haines to the rest of southeast Alaska and beyond. The only road out of Haines runs north, into the Yukon Territory and, eventually, back into Alaska if you go one way at the junction with the Alaska Highway, or all the way through Canada and down to the Lower Forty-eight if you go the other.

Two, or was that three steps forward? It was time for one more step back.

Deciding to award a new tour permit for a Skagway-based outdoor excursion company operating at Glacier Point, across the inlet and down about five miles from my house, was not as easy. It took a few more meetings to resolve, for all kinds of important reasons, from former guides' revelations about the tour company's lack of safety equipment and poor maintenance and training to the potential environmental impact.

LAST SEPTEMBER, I floated down the Kongakut River way up in the far northeastern edge of Alaska near the Beaufort Sea in a rubber raft with five strangers from the Lower Forty-eight and two Haines guides. I wanted to see for myself what the threatened Arctic National Wildlife Refuge looked like. I had never been north of the Arctic Circle before. It was not covered in ice and snow, and it wasn't a vast swamp full of mosquitoes that no one would want to visit anyway, as some proponents of drilling argue. It looked to me like the earth must have when it was new and no one lived here yet. It was easy to imagine woolly mammoths and dinosaurs stepping out from behind a bend in the river.

It was a little terrifying to be in such a small party in such a big place. I'm used to broad vistas and high mountains and camping in a wall tent during moose season up the Chilkat River. I am outdoorsy and capable, but this was Alaska on a whole new scale. There were wide, wide valleys and weighty mountains made of rock, with few to no trees, and miles and miles of tundra carpets in all shades of early autumn's red, gold, brown, and green. The river was as clear as the Tenakee hot spring and a lot colder. Grayling and char swam below us, abundant and as bright as tropical fish in an aquarium.

We hiked on the ancient caribou migration trails grooved a foot deep into the hillsides. We saw bears and wolves in the distance, and once a bull caribou, all by himself, and a playful fox in one camp. It was so quiet. I whispered instead of singing when I wandered alone on the bluff above our tents. None of us did much talking except at mealtimes. This was not a place where you'd climb out of your sleeping bag in the morning and say to yourself, *I'd like to live here*; rather you think, *I'm lucky to be passing through sacred territory and I better tread lightly so as to leave it as I found it.* I stood and stared a lot. Sometimes the scenery was too much to take in all at once, and when that happened, I focused on paddling if we were on the move, or on the objects at my feet if we had stopped to wander. I searched the pebbled stream banks for granite rocks or black limestone with the white ghosts of fossilized coral and shells embedded in them from a long-ago time when that land was at the bottom of the sea in another part of the world before the giant plates of the earth crust shifted. Before the mountains were made.

I had brought along Margaret "Mardy" Murie's classic Alaskan memoir *Two in the Far North*, which I am embarrassed to admit

I had never read before. She was great company and the perfect tent partner when the night winds and the wolves' howls made me afraid to sleep. She had been in this part of Alaska in 1926, camping and traveling for an entire summer with her researcher husband and their baby. A baby! And she seemed so normal, preparing meals for the next day after the baby was asleep for the night, writing in her diary, watching the clouds and worrying, too, sometimes, when she was left alone in their camp. The scenery and wildlife she describes were the same ones I saw, thanks in large part to her efforts to create the Arctic National Wildlife Refuge way back in 1960, before most Alaskans, much less Americans, realized what a treasure this land was, or even suspected the Arctic would ever need protection from human development. From the first sentence of her book, "What, after all, are the most precious things in a life?" I knew I had made a literary friend. She was speaking right to me.

So I answered her. "This place, Alaska, and the people I love."

Reading down the page, I found *her* answer to be more eloquent but the same in sentiment, although she had foreseen contemporary Alaskan concerns:

> My prayer is that Alaska will not lose the heart-nourishing friendliness of her youth—that her people will always care for one another, her towns remain friendly and not completely ruled by the dollar—and that her great wild places will remain great, and wild, and free, where wolf and caribou, wolverine and grizzly bear, and all the arctic blossoms may live in the delicate balance which supported them long before impetuous man appeared in the North.

This, she said, is Alaska's value, our gift to the "harassed" world.

"You should see it now," I told her. "Mardy, you have no idea how right you were," I said to the thin nylon tent, her book in my hand.

BEFORE THE ASSEMBLY meeting, as I read the letters and emails, pro and con, about the Glacier Point tour permit, and answered phone calls and my door, a winter's worth of ice was leaving the Chilkat River. Huge white and crystal-blue slabs drifted past my window at low tide, like empty royal barges with spirit passengers. My friend Betty has been watching them, too, and also what she says are children in old-fashioned bright skirts and blouses dancing on the shore as they pass. The doctor thinks she is hallucinating. When I asked her if she saw other things besides children, she said there is a black cat that visits her, and a young man appeared on the lawn when she was filling her bird feeder. I asked her if he bothered her, and she said, "No, he was friendly." When the doctor said he was taking away her driver's license because she was seeing things that weren't there, she countered with "How do you know? You can't see love and you can't see hate, but they are real."

In India, they set candles in paper vessels and strew flowers and cremated remains of loved ones on a stretch of the Ganges some call the river of death. The Chilkat is my river of life. It has witnessed, as Neil Young sings, all my changes. It has flowed past and through moments large and small, parties and funerals, in all kinds of weather and many different moods. It's always there to walk beside. My children were raised here and now my grandchildren swing on the old swings and ride bikes in circles down the paths between the roses, always with the moving water near. My backyard, which isn't a yard at all or for that matter all "mine," is a three-mile stretch of public land that is level and easy to walk on adjacent to where the Chilkat River meets the sea. It's part forest, part beach, part meadow, part river, part ocean, and at low tide, part mudflats. It's a popular place to walk a dog, bird-watch, or just sit on a log and look around for a while. Popular is relative. There are times in any given day that I'm the only one on the beach, and times when there may be dozens of people, depending on the weather and the day of the week. Sunday afternoons are the busiest.

Haines is a town of people and a wilderness that's home to bears—both smaller black bears, and large Alaskan brown bears—and wolves, moose, goats, birds, and sea life. The boundary of Glacier Bay National Park and Preserve runs along the ridge across from my house, and that parkland is connected to Canada's Tatshenshini-Alsek and Kluane parks, and they bump up against Alaska's Wrangell-St. Elias National Park, creating one huge international wilderness area with millions of acres and miles and miles of protected land. If I look out my back door in the morning all I see are mountains and valleys and the water. If I look out my front door, I might catch a glimpse of the yellow school bus through the spruce trees on its way to pick up kids down the road.

Glacier Point is a broad flat fan of trees and meadows in front of the Davidson Glacier and the small lake made by the water tumbling underneath it in a short river to the inlet, about five miles south of my house on the opposite shore. Tourists have been coming to see the glacier for a hundred and fifty years. There are no roads to Glacier Point, and while I can see it in the distance from our beach, the point is not a regular destination for most of us. You have to take a boat, for starters, and it's far enough that the wind and waves can build up, and weather can pin you there for longer than you planned to stay. There are less than a handful of private cabins; sometimes local kayakers paddle over and spend a day or camp overnight.

The tour company that owns a couple hundred acres there was already bringing fifteen thousand tourists a year over, primarily from Skagway-docked cruise ships via fast shuttle boats. The tourists hike and ride all-terrain buses from the beached boats up to the glacier view lake, and paddle across it in large fiberglass canoes, assisted by outboard motors. Glacier Point and the lake is a beautiful place and, for many, the visit is a life-changing experience. I brought my Aunt Jeanne from New York on the canoe tour when another company owned it. Even though it sounds hokey to many locals, I loved it, mainly because my urban, elderly aunt could not stop smiling at the icebergs, the muddy outfall from the glacier, the lupine, columbine, and lilies. Poking around inside the blue ice cave under the glacier was magical. In the old photos at the museum, the glacier reaches halfway out into the inlet. We used to see the tip of its white tongue on the point from our beach, but now the glacier's head has retreated into the mountainside like a turtle's into its shell.

ON THE NIGHT of the permit decision–making meeting, the tour company owner arrived from Skagway with a boatload of employees and friends and family members who filled the assembly chambers. A Haines tourism pioneer spoke in favor of the tour, as did the president of our largest tour company. They urged a compromise; "mitigate rather than eliminate" was their plea. Opponents reiterated their complaints about the company's mismanagement. Local fishermen said the tour's shuttles ran over their nets, which was bad enough, but then refused to compensate them.

I asked the tour company president, who had already promised to remedy every single concern raised right away—he practically opened his checkbook to pay for past damage to the fishing fleet on the spot—what he planned to do about the additional human waste, since his current system of dumping barrels from the out-houses into a pit in the woods didn't seem to be very sanitary, and doubling the number of guests and guides using it would make it worse. He said he was building a brand-new septic system with flush toilets.

"When will it be completed?" I asked.

"Tomorrow," he promised.

Could he have possibly thought that I would not know that the ground was still frozen and that there was still snow in the north-facing woods where the sun hasn't penetrated? Had he been out for a walk around here lately?

In every country, state, community, there is a core value, a heritage and an enduring identity that makes that particular place and those particular people what and who they are. Some, like Rome or the Swiss Alps, are not only local treasures but global ones as well. I live in a place that is on par with such wonders. I am a borough assembly member, too. Part of my responsibility is to make sure that nothing harms our way of life, our pride and joy, for future generations. If we didn't have a river rich in salmon and full of wildlife, a proposed mine would not be such a big concern. But we do. If we don't preserve the beautiful places to see and experience here, we won't have tourists, and we need them to help a lot of people here make a living. They come by the thousands to gently float through the Chilkat Bald Eagle Preserve in rubber rafts, to ski on mountains accessible only by helicopter and that will never have chairlifts or lodges, to see wild bears catching salmon, and to cruise the fjords and straits of the Inside Passage alongside humpback and killer whales.

But of course there's a rub. How many tourists are too many? That question and what they can do on their visit remains partially up to us. Borough Code requires assembly approval for new tour permits. I was a visitor in the Arctic. Without my guides and the rafting company's permits to float the Kongakut, I would never have seen it, and because of that trip I returned home with a new appreciation for it. Love is not too strong a word for what I felt at first sight, and so I had fired off an email to Lisa Murkowski asking her to please keep oil companies away from the Arctic National Wildlife Refuge and the coastal plain of the Refuge's migrating caribou herds. Yet, because I took that tour, I altered the landscape. I crushed the delicate alpine mosses that cushioned my sleeping bag and pad each night. The bush plane broke the silence and shot dust and gravel on the makeshift runway when the pilot arrived to shuttle us back to Arctic Village, Fort Yukon, and finally Fairbanks. Did we remember to remove the neon strips of flagging tape we tied to the willows so he'd find us or are they still flapping in the wind up there? Will the next group's trip be diminished because we've been there already? Will the bear we saw on the riverbank find another stream to fish in, one where it won't be disturbed? Yet if Alaskans don't share our special places with other people who appreciate them, multinational corporations may strip them bare.

Debra recommended that the assembly approve the tour permit but with conditions, including abiding by a safety equipment plan outlined by the borough EMT, and another plan to protect the Arctic and Caspian tern colonies on the point. They nest on the ground. ATV riders would have to avoid them. Stephanie added another condition limiting the tour to eight thousand guests a season (the company had requested fifteen thousand, the same as my canoe tour had) and requiring a review in the fall to decide whether or not to renew the permit. I insisted the septic system had to be completed. I had no idea how the borough would enforce that, or any of these conditions. Glacier Point inspections would be a logistical challenge—remember, getting there requires a sturdy boat and at best half a workday. Could borough officials even show up and inspect a business on private property? The forests and meadows between the glacier and the lake and the beach and the inlet were once homesteaded, and remain privately owned, although largely undeveloped. We had never required this with any other tour permit.

One of the last members of the public to speak was the most colorful. Literally. Jojo, who volunteers on the radio and helps coach the swim team, wore a multihued knit hat, a long flowery skirt, and a bright top that revealed the pretty pinks, blues, and greens of a large tattoo on her arm. She reminded us that she did not think the company operated in a safe manner. Then she quoted Glacier Bay author Kim Heacox from *The Only Kayak*, a memoir about his life in a small community over the mountains on the edge of the bay. The beauty of Alaska was meant to overwhelm us, he wrote, and was "not for us to overwhelm" with development, industry and too many people. He calls for "restraint and respect" to keep Alaska's jewels from becoming amusement parks. Moments earlier, in an effort to convince the assembly of his commitment to creating a world-class attraction in Haines, the tour company owner had said his hero was Walt Disney and that he wanted the Glacier Point experience for tourists to replicate Disney's Frontierland theme park.

Aldo Leopold wrote that the undoing of the planet began with the "tyranny" of small decisions. I feel so helpless in response to the news of rising sea levels, melting polar ice, storms, fires, and floods. The Chilkat River king salmon are threatened now, and limits are being placed by the Alaska Department of Fish and Game on when they are caught and by whom. The commercial fleet must avoid certain waters to allow the kings safe passage to the spawning grounds.

I couldn't divert every overflowing culvert with a pickax, no matter how much fun I had doing it.

But I could vote no to a new tour in a beautiful place because I had a bad feeling about its management. It's one thing to share Alaska with visitors. It's another to encourage them to treat her roughly. There are trade-offs between enjoying the wild and preserving it. The argument was made that because of its historic uses—parts of Glacier Point were also logged at one time—that it didn't matter what tourists did over there. Let the folks have their fun. The canoes on my tour were not exactly natural, it's true. But their negative impact is minimal (as long they are operated safely) and judging by my aunt's reaction, worth it. However, it is immoral to encourage thousands of people to come to Alaska to zoom around in circles in exhaust-belching ATVs just for kicks in the shadow of a glacier that's rapidly receding because of the effects of global warming caused by burning fossil fuels. It's worse than fiddling while Rome burns.

I did not say all that in the meeting, because it would draw the kind of red line that would prevent future tour permit applicants from considering my views. It would not be helpful to anyone and was not necessary. Jojo would have cheered, but she was already on the glacier's side, and mine. Three of us voted against the permit, and three were for it, with the conditions. The mayor broke the tie in favor of allowing the tour to go ahead. In retrospect, I regret not requiring the ATVs to be fueled by solar-powered batteries.

THERE WAS NOTHING as morally challenging as a tour permit application or as physically satisfying as breaking up an ice jam on another afternoon's walk. Instead, a soft gray mist had settled over the river and shoreline and the mountains stood guard above the bands of fog, their tops dusted in the last, I hoped, of the snow flurries. They, along with the wide thawing mudflats in the silver light, created an Ansel Adams–style landscape that could have been titled *Yosemite-by-the-Sea*. It was the sort of day when all is right with the world even if its politics have disappointed me. "After you have exhausted what there is in business, politics, conviviality, love, and so on—have found that none of these finally satisfy, or permanently wear—what remains? Nature remains . . ." Walt Whitman wrote. He's right.

I cannot stay too long in a dark mood in this particular place. It won't let me. I should be angry or worried about the future, but not now, and not here. Soon, May will charge up the Chilkat. The first smelts we call hooligans, and their entourage of feeding sea lions, seals, and shorebirds will sing to the backbeat of the melting streams and rising river. Bears will splash for their breakfasts and chew up intestine-clearing greens. Soon the salmon—kings, sockeye, pinks, chum, and coho—will follow. In November and December some three thousand eagles, one of the largest gatherings in the world, descend on the snowy river flats near Klukwan to feed on what's left of the spawning salmon concentrated in warm, naturally occurring pools in the otherwise frozen channels twenty miles upstream from where I stand. Everyone and everything contribute to the well-being of the Chilkat Valley.

I would love to tell you that on this watercolor-kind-of-morning I am as much a part of the scene as that weathered white jawbone of last summer's salmon stuck in the tide line detritus, a few of its teeth still attached, and that the raven's cry didn't startle me a minute ago. I would like to be as tuned in to this day and this place as a poet or a Native wise woman, or Mardy Murie and her baby in their tent by a lake with no name in who-knows-where. I have eaten my weight in salmon every year for the past thirty. My Native neighbors would say my very flesh and blood should be mostly salmon by now, which should make me part of all this, too, right?

Yet today, after all my talk about "reading" the Chilkat, I missed a wolf. A wolf! They are rare on this side of the river, so near town. After we came home, Chip said he saw that the dogs and I walked within stick-tossing distance of a large black wolf. We never suspected we had company. I am a total failure in the mindful-walking department. You'd think the dogs would have at least caught the scent.

I do know in my own not-so-brittle bones that nature can save us if we let her. When I returned from a Seattle nursing home, broken-bodied and afraid I'd never walk again after my 2005 cycling accident, and my children and Chip helped me into a bed by the living room windows, it was also springtime. They had put in the screens and the sashes were up. I could breathe the sweet, cool, scented air, and hear the waves and the birds and the wind. You can tell me it was the morphine talking, but you'd be wrong. I swear that the river rafted my spirit, and my body, back to health.

I can hop off the porch so effortlessly I have forgotten how much practice it took after I'd begun to take those first steps on uneven ground toward the beach and dig my boots in the damp sand and lower myself with a crutch down onto a soft gray log. I don't forget how happy that made me. These days the joy I find in waking up in this wonderful world is plenty. My good fortune, luck, grace—it slays me. It is a new day and I am in it, as Mary Oliver would say. That's why I had been humming my own show tune, "These little town blues, are melting away . . . I want to be a part of it . . . " substituting "Chilkat, Chilkat" for "New York, New York" when I totally missed the wolf. It's not that I wasn't paying attention—I was celebrating. And I want to believe that wolf was, too. He didn't run away when he heard and saw us, did he? We can't leave it up to poets to save this world for us. Politicians and business leaders, priests and preschool teachers, you and me, too, had better do all in our power to make sure that nature remains for as long as rivers flow to the sea. Our lives depend on it.

IIIIIIIIIIIIIIIIIIIIIIIIIIIIIIIIIIIIIIIIIIIIIIIIIIIIIIIIIIIIIIIIIIIIIIIIIIIIIIIIIIIIIIIIIIIIIIIIIIIIII
Manager and Committee Reports:

At the Chilkat Center, Strength and Stretch is on a hiatus for the summer, but Yoga and Tai Chi continue.

Parks & Rec discussed a suitable site for the Mosquito Lake outhouse and is researching a maintenance agreement. Funding remains an obstacle. They will hold a trails workshop at the library next week.

It will be a busy construction season with harbor expansion, wastewater treatment plant upgrade, new preschool, and the facilities shop upgrade. Southeast Roadbuilders is holding a pre-construction meeting on the Haines Airport upgrade next week.

Lifeguard Jordan Stigen has resigned to attend college this fall. Early Bird swimmers especially will miss her.

The new sand truck has been ordered.

IIIIIIIIIIIIIIIIIIIIIIIIIIIIIIIIIIIIIIIIIIIIIIIIIIIIIIIIIIIIIIIIIIIIIIIIIIIIIIIIIIIIIIIIIIIIIIIIIIIIII

FIFTEEN

Granny's Got Another Gear

FOR MY SIXTIETH birthday I bought myself a custom-made bicycle. It took about two months to build and arrived a few weeks before my party. It's dark green with a tan leather Brooks seat and matching handlebar tape. There are chrome fenders and spoked wheels. It has the same fit and gearing as my old racing bike but is disguised as a more classic cruiser. Known as a randonneur or "rando"-style bike, it's designed for the over-two-hundred-kilometer races and relatively fast group rides of the same name. I told the designer, whose name is Smiley, that I want to be riding it when I'm a hundred, and he added a "granny gear," a third chain ring, to make sure I can always climb Cemetery Hill.

I love cycling in Haines, but the weather can be a problem. It rains and storms and is often windy. The bike has a waterproof box on the handlebars that can keep my assembly papers dry. It can also hold snacks to share, or a sandwich and a drink if I decide to eat lunch at Chilkoot Lake before pedaling home. I am usually in too much of a hurry for snacking or lunch, though. My new bike also has a headlight and a taillight and, best of all, a little brass bell to alert the bears with a loud yet pleasing *ping-ping*. Chip says it sounds like an ice cream truck. Lately the hot weather makes me wish there were one in Haines.

The bike is built for the long haul and I have survived one. I'm nearing the end of my three-year term on the assembly. In a few weeks I will take yet another long haul—a 350-mile cycling trip up the Haines Highway into Canada, over the Chilkat Pass, and on to Whitehorse, back down through the White Pass and along the Klondike Highway to Skagway, and return home by ferry. I'm traveling with two friends, my next-door neighbor, Fran, and Kate, a river guide who has spent her summers in Haines for longer than I have lived here. Both women are a few years older than I am and are seasoned campers, though not as avid cyclists. We plan to take our time, completing the trip in about a week. This will be not only the first long ride on my new bike, but my first overnight bicycle camping trip, ever. I can't wait.

A few days before my birthday party, on a warm sunny June afternoon, I headed out alone on my new bike, just to see how she rolled out on Mud Bay Road and to think about life at six decades, and the place I've spent the majority of them in. There was a cruise ship in town, with more passengers and crew on board than Haines has residents, and I knew that they were still repaving the road in front of the school. The mother bears are back at the Chilkoot River, along with this spring's cubs, waiting for the salmon to arrive, and I don't like to go out there by myself, even with my new bell. I chose to ride in the opposite direction from town first, over the hill and past Beth's retreat center. I usually work out early in the morning with Chip and we rarely see anyone, so it was fun to catch the cyclist in front of me and discover it was Teresa. She had a new road bike, too, an Italian Bianchi she had bought from a friend and was learning how to ride it. She wasn't ready for the hills and was making loops on the two miles of flat blacktop along the waterfront between Mount Riley and the cannery.

I'd hardly seen her in a month and it was nice to visit. It was eighty degrees, which to Alaskans might as well be a hundred, so I didn't mind the slower pace. "Make sure you drink plenty of water," Mother Teresa said. "And I hope you are wearing sunscreen." She had a pre-cancerous spot taken off her lip last year. The reason we hadn't seen each other recently was because I had been busy with assembly and committee meetings, Stoli had a baby boy in April (his sisters had been at my house more), and Pearl had surgery on both her back legs (I was nursing her back to health). Instead of meeting Teresa at our regular noon yoga class at the Chilkat Center, I'd been making peanut butter sandwiches and chocolate milk for granddaughters Silvia Rose and Lani, and then walking Pearl on a leash slowly down the path and back to their house. I'd had book writing deadlines, too, and obituaries—people don't stop dying just because I have other obligations.

While my house was dusty and my yard overgrown, Teresa had been sprucing up her home and garden for a special guest. In a few weeks her son would see where she lived for the first time. We were all getting used to the idea that she had a child who was actually a grown man with two young adult children. Teresa has grandkids! After all the years of praying to St. Anthony to "look around for something lost that can't be found," she had found the one thing she thought she had lost forever. She had reunited with the baby she had as a teenager. "Miracles do happen," she told me again, still amazed at her good fortune. Better still, his name is Tony. She gave him up for adoption over fifty years ago when she was an unwed teenager. Her parents were devout Catholics—as Teresa is today—and "it was a different time." She would not have been able to provide him with all he needed for the kind of life she hoped he would have, she said.

Teresa had privately prayed for her baby since his birth so many years ago, but it was a secret until she took a DNA test on an ancestry website as part of her quest for dual American–Italian citizenship and, she confessed, checking the share information box, in part to see if he was out there somewhere. At the time, nothing turned up. A few years later, though, with the encouragement of his wife, Tony took a test, too, and Teresa popped up as a parent match. They emailed, then spoke on the phone, then Facetimed with the rest of her family—her husband, Larry, and their adult children, Lyndsey and Nik—before she broke the news to friends. Last winter Teresa and Larry took a road trip and reconnected with Tony's other mother, Joyce, who had been Teresa's nurse during childbirth. That was an emotional and joyous reunion, too. So much could have gone wrong. Instead it was all very right. Sometimes there are happy endings.

Ten years from now I won't remember the specifics of yesterday's assembly meeting, but I will always remember the day a year ago when Teresa told me about Tony during a hike up Mount Riley and how scared and happy she was, and how we brushed off the tears, and how we agreed that this was not the time for what-ifs and should-haves or could-haves, or even to sift through the choices that have delivered her, and them, and all of us to this place and time. What mattered was now, not then. Tony's wife, the grandkids, they all love Teresa, as well as her family, and it's mutual. Now they are coming here, and Teresa is refinishing her floor and her kitchen cabinets. She reupholstered the sofa, too.

I was so happy to bump into Teresa and be pedaling along beside her, next to the blue-green inlet, the crab pot buoys bobbing, the red cannery on pilings, the mountains beyond, the warm breeze, as we talked about how familiar Tony is, his eyes, his face, and all the ways he is like her, and her other children. I asked her to describe him. He's tall, a golfer, a businessman, a husband, a father, "he's extremely family oriented," considerate and kind, Catholic—and he gave her flowers. "Tony is sort of serious," she said. "Stoic might be the right word, or steady might be better," and I teased her about whether, then, she was sure he was *her* son, and she said, "Heather, I prayed about him for fifty years in secret. Trust me, I may not show it, but I can be stoic." If we hadn't been on bikes, I would have kissed her.

Before we parted—Teresa was heading home and I had a few more places to go—I promised I'd have her new, old, big family over for a beach party when Tony arrived. As I rode away, I hummed the Lucinda Williams song "Compassion," after a poem her father, Miller Williams, wrote. The poet and his daughter reminded me to have compassion for everyone I met, "even if they don't want it," because no one can see the pain we all carry down "where the spirit meets the bone." I remembered how Teresa said I should be careful about quoting literature when we were campaigning, but after nearly a whole term on the assembly I have found something I lost, too, the confidence to be who I am and say what I feel.

I don't wear earbuds, as I like the sounds of my ride as much as the sights and the thoughts that come in and out of my head and heart on the wind. When I want to hear a song, I make my own music. You know me well enough by now to realize I have a sort of soundtrack to my life. Carols, show tunes, country. While the words to "Compassion" were perfect for how I was feeling, the tune is kind of a dirge so I switched to "Bring Me Sunshine," an old song that Willie Nelson recorded a version of that the Haines A Cappella Women's Chorus sings. "Be light hearted, all day long," I sang to no one and everyone, "keep me singing happy songs." I thought about how everybody was dealing with something. I didn't even know my oldest friend had a hole in her heart all these years. It's important to remember, I told myself, that sometimes, like for Teresa, what was lost can be found.

I'VE LOST PLENTY of things while I've served on the assembly that St. Anthony may or may not be able to recover for me: sleep, glasses, balance, pens, trust, travel mugs, my temper, my place on the iPad while searching for a line in the Borough Code, and hardest of all, one of the great loves of my life: this community. That's what it felt like during the recall. My friend Beth told me once that when something or someone you love dies, it leaves a kind of cave in your chest. For a while it's a cold dark place, but slowly it begins to fill up again with warm, light things, a laugh with a friend, a meal with the kids, a walk with grandchildren and an old dog. A thank you. A kiss. A nice bike ride and a sunny day like today. I'm glad that I didn't quit the assembly, or Haines, when I was tempted to, and instead did what I have been doing since I was a child: kept pedaling. That helped me understand where I came from and discover where I'd like to go.

The recall hit me much harder than it did Tresham or Tom. Rather than assume that they had let people down, they, correctly now I see, knew that they had done and said exactly what the voters hoped they would and, more importantly, what they believed was right. Tom fought back. Tresham was unconcerned. Me? Well, you know I was a wreck. I was still thinking I needed to be a good hostess, and that the borough assembly was meeting in my living room and I was passing a tray of sandwiches, drinks, and something interesting to read. I was playing the part of the peace-making mother cautioning her children not to hit one another. I believed, in some place deep inside me from years of learning my lessons well, that I should be the "lady" in the room. I heard my high school field hockey coach admonishing us that Friends Academy girls do not lower ourselves to the other team's games if they play rough. We rise above it. And I heard my grandmother's voice from the grave lecturing that if I can't say something nice, then don't say anything at all.

Is this what other women holding office have to overcome? Or maybe women in any occupation or difficult situation? What is this expectation that we should make everything okay and everyone comfortable? I can't tell you how many obituaries I've written where the widow, or mother, or daughter greets me at the door, thanks me for coming, pours me some fresh coffee, and offers me the best chair at the table in the middle of her worst hard time.

During the recall, Julia, who is a doctor, told me she thought I was being singled out by the men like Big Don and his bunch because I was vulnerable. Because I was a woman. I had not wanted to believe that and pointed to Tom and Tresham. But the image I had of what a good woman is and what my role on the assembly should be was limited by my own upbringing and assumptions. I wasn't seeing the whole picture. Maybe I had even misinterpreted

Stephanie's advice about seeing the assembly chambers as my living room. Treating it as my home might really mean making *my* rules and not allowing myself to be taken advantage of. All these years, I had been emboldening Big Don by never saying, no, this is not a good time, by inviting him in and offering him coffee while I was still in my pajamas, even by giving him my book and being so happy he liked it.

Did he know that I would be the most affected by his petition? Did he assume I'd quit in the face of his relentless pressure? Had I become the lightning rod for his discontent because I allowed him to upset me in a way that the men he targeted hadn't? My guess is yes. It may have not been calculated, but I was easy prey. I had always advised my daughters that, to paraphrase Eleanor Roosevelt, no one could make them feel inferior without their permission, but I had not taken that lesson to my own heart. No wonder he persisted. I never resisted because I wanted to be open-minded and fair, but mainly because I didn't want to be rude.

Ever since my eleventh birthday, when my parents gave me a brand new Royce Union one-speed bicycle and I wheeled past the house hollering, "Look, Mom, no hands!" I have always wanted to please everyone so badly that I don't always watch where I am going. Back then, I hit a street sign. I insisted I was fine, but was I really? I still have the scar on my knee. Whenever I came home from school and told my mother that I had gotten a big part in the play, or that I threw the softball farther than any of the girls and most of the boys at field day, she'd always ask, "What about the other children? Did anyone else have a good day?" What I heard was, "That's nice, but if you work harder, you'll do better," and that my feelings were not as important as acknowledging theirs. I can't say why, as I don't think it was her intention to teach me to be considerate to a fault. She herself was a strong woman who seemed to me to do exactly as she pleased, but perhaps she, like many women I know, had absorbed the lessons of our culture and passed them on to her daughters to help us survive in what remains a man's world. Who knew politics would force me to confront an existential crisis?

As A KID, I kept pedaling harder because if I slowed down, I'd fall over. As the years went by my instinct to keep going served me well, to a degree, and soon my feet were clipped into pedals of swifter bikes. Then, thanks to a random accident—a driver went through a stop sign—*bam*, I was down. I was hit by that truck about fifteen years ago now, while riding another favorite new bicycle. Then, my children, friends, and doctors were sure I would never ride again. It took about two years to regain my strength, inside and out. My rehab involved walking in the pool, as well as a lot of physical therapy. As soon as I was able, I began swimming and secretly set out to complete a mile, never mind that I couldn't kick yet and needed to squeeze a float between my knees.

When I finally did it, I told Marnie, my physical therapist, how well I was doing, expecting her praise. Instead she asked, "Is it your goal to be a swimmer?" And I said, no, not really. I wanted to walk my dogs and hike to the top of Mount Riley—and she said, okay, walk to your next appointment. Her office was two and a half miles from my house. It took me two hours and I needed to call Chip for a ride home because I was so sore.

When I could walk to her office in under forty-five minutes, I began to focus on what I really wanted: to ride my bike again, fast, and far. And even as I said it, I knew a lot of people would tell me not to, and many would think I was crazy, and I didn't care. A few years later, after Chip and I won the one hundred and fifty mile local bike race as a two-person team, Marnie said something else to me. She had recently been through a rough patch herself and ended a long-term relationship. When I praised her for being the nicest, most caring person I knew, she laughed. She said she wasn't *that* nice. She used to try to be all things to all people, but now she doesn't anymore, and she's a lot happier. The thing is, I would never have guessed if she hadn't told me. The shift was inside, not outside.

Buddhists advise dying a little every day as a way to learn to live the way we are meant to. The bike wreck was my first taste of being near death, and it was mostly physical. The recall was my second, and it was mostly emotional. But after the initial shock, I have kept pedaling—because I'm good at it, because it is fun, and because in this, I can ride with the boys and even beat them. Also, I have a good partner, in cycling and in life. Chip wakes me up every summer morning to ride with him, and never condescends to my gender. He assumes I can ride as well as he can. He also pushes me to have more faith in myself, and he encouraged me to buy my new Rando, as I call her. (She's definitely a woman—a strong, handsome, and practical one of a certain age with some flash and sass.)

I bought new red suede bike shoes to go with her, because I have always wanted to wear red shoes but I have big feet, size eleven, and used to think I shouldn't call attention to them. My new shoes have metal cleats on the sole that clip into the pedals, but unlike my racing shoes, they are built for easy transitioning from the pedals to the trail or a sidewalk. They lace up and look like fancy sneakers. At an intersection on Main Street, I pulled up to the stop sign, unclipped, and walked the bike down the sidewalk.

Becky Nash stopped her car in the middle of the street and rolled down her window. She had two of her grandsons in the back seat and a box of quilting fabric in the front. A truck behind her honked and she said, "What's your hurry?" to the rearview mirror as he drove around us. She asked how our newest grandbaby is doing and about my daughter JJ's new job in Juneau. She's moving back there from Unalaska to be a principal closer to home. Another car went around Becky and she waved. I reminded her about my birthday party potluck this weekend and she replied that Don is fishing and she'll be in Sweden visiting her sister, but we can celebrate next time we are all together. "I'm taking Noah with me this time." After Aaron's death, his little boy has been spending a lot of time with Becky and Don.

Becky has made a positive impact in my home as well. It happened a little after the recall petition signers' names were made public. She dropped by while I was out running errands. At the dairy case, I had bumped into a woman who'd signed the petition, and I was so upset that I had left the store without buying any groceries and returned to find a note from Becky on the counter. She proposed we both get tattoos, which she had designed.

I called her up to see if she was serious. She said she would be right over to do mine and then she'd put on hers, and all we needed to decide was whose would be green and whose would be red.

How big would they be and where would mine go, I asked?

"I know the perfect place. I think it will fit there," she said.

Becky is an excellent seamstress and knows her needles, and she's a nurse. But when did she learn how to tattoo? "I don't think this is a good idea," I said.

She said to open the drawer in my kitchen's workbench island.

There I saw two rolls of what looked like contact paper. They were about four feet long and six inches wide. "Be Kind, Be Brave, Be Thankful" was printed on them with transferable red and green letters. I used to think this message was about how to treat others; now I know that it is also advice for the way I care for myself.

"They're 'wall tattoos,'" she said.

Together we put the green one up on the fir panel above my pantry door, teetering on wobbly chairs, using Becky's wooden ruler and my dull carpenter's pencil and counting the inches so it would be centered—measuring wrong twice—before rubbing the letters off the backing with a credit card.

I love it. What if we had parted over Trump? A corollary to the adage that politics is the art of the possible is: don't permit politics to make friendship impossible.

BEFORE RIDING HOME, I tucked the bike in the rack by the door of the borough office and went in to check my assembly mail. The new front desk person, the first face you see when you walk in (we don't say receptionist anymore, and technically she isn't one, but rather an assistant to the planning department) smiled at me and nodded hello. I snagged a piece of candy from her dish and she said to enjoy the sunshine and I told her that I wished that she could, too. She smiled and shrugged. I know I am a lucky woman to have choices, even if I don't always make the best ones.

Back outside, I stopped to drink from my water bottle and looked around. I saw the inlet from the hill above our lumberyard. The view never grows old. My ride around town today could be the front page of a brochure on the most scenic bike rides in America.

Again, I thought about how there were times in the past three years when I wanted to move. Of course, every day isn't like this one. Haines isn't all sunshine and light. Public service isn't, either.

When I finally pulled into my driveway, I walked my new bike down the gravel rather than risk a skid and scratch its beautiful paint or my knees. I smelled the wild roses and heard the kids next door—my daughters and grandchildren had been swimming at the pond down the road and must be back. The weathered old smokehouse could use some TLC. I hadn't smoked salmon and canned it since joining the assembly. This summer, for the first time, I didn't plant my garden, either. It has been too hard to keep up with. The farmers market is full of local produce, though, so we haven't been without it, and one of my sons-in-law is a fisherman who keeps us supplied with fresh salmon and more for the freezer. Stephanie brings me flowers from her garden once a week.

When my children were young, I vowed that after they were grown and the mortgage was paid, I would buy myself a sports car for my fiftieth birthday, thinking at the time that was when I would be *really* old. It would be a 1968 classic MG, British-racing-green convertible with tan leather seats and chrome-spoked wheels. I wished, then, to become the kind of old woman who drove a sports car in Alaska. As you can tell, my new ride has some of that dream in her. I'm young enough to love riding a bike, and old enough to know I'm not a sports car person. I guess I never was. It's taken me almost sixty years to finally understand that at my core, and unapologetically, I'm a pedaler.

To be hopeful in bad times is not just foolishly romantic. . . . And if we do act, in however small a way, we don't have to wait for some grand utopian future. The future is an infinite succession of presents, and to live now as we think human beings should live, in defiance of all that is bad around us, is itself a marvelous victory.

—HOWARD ZINN

SIXTEEN

Home Safe

WHEN I TOLD my daughter JJ that I planned to write about what happened when I ran for local office and won, she said "Are you sure? It's been a pretty traumatic experience for you."

Well, there's that.

Ken, an old pilot friend who left Haines years ago but still subscribes to the paper, asked me on a recent visit here if I had "found the good" on the borough assembly, echoing the title of one of my books.

"Yes," I said, surprising him.

"Glad to hear it," he said. I was, too. I hadn't realized how I felt until he asked me. It is very good to live in a community where people are engaged, where we participate in our government, and care enough to speak out passionately about local issues.

As my term draws to a close, I think more about some of the "marvelous" moments, large and small, as Howard Zinn writes. Like the first time we voted unanimously, and every time after that. We passed budgets and negotiated successfully with the local Public Employees Union, without any of the drama or threats to shut down the government that often accompany these issues in the nation and state capitals. Property values have risen, and the taxes have stayed about the same in two budget cycles but are going up this year due to cuts by our new governor. A tobacco tax was instituted. A plastic bag ban is in place. One year we made sure kids under eighteen could swim for free at the pool. The next year, due to more state budget cuts, we didn't. Nothing is for certain. Yet, applications for liquor licenses have been approved, gender neutral updates have been made to the Code, we bought a new police car, and we've debated the allocation of funds to support local nonprofits such as the Haines Friends of Recycling's hazardous waste collection program, the swim team, the Haines Animal Rescue Kennel, and Becky's Place, a shelter for victims of domestic violence. One year we budgeted $65,000 for nonprofits, and another year less overall, but in a more strategic way to help where it was needed the most.

We decided to beef up the planning department, but nixed the idea of using a drone to check for violations after residents threatened to shoot it out of the sky. We spent a lot of time on commercial tour permit applications, and no one is happy about that. We still haven't solved the problems with the preferred heli-ski zones map or with bears and people along the Chilkoot River, but we do have a moratorium on any new tours out there until we can make it safer.

There have been funny meetings, especially when it came to creating ordinances for the budding (pardon the pun) marijuana business, now that it is legal in Alaska. Haines has several growers, and a pot shop, or dispensary, as they are called. "Now you say that the waste from the plants will be composted. Can bears get high if they forage in it?" "When you say edibles, what does that mean? Pot brownies?" Some assembly members knew exactly how much an ounce of pot costs, others had no clue. During one meeting we all got the giggles, in an I-can't-believe-we-are-talking-about-this in-public-much-less-at-an-assembly-meeting-and-it's-*okay* way.

IN TOWN YESTERDAY I saw that my books were in the window of the bookstore, which has a new owner. The colorful and earnest young Jojo bought it. I also bumped into Kyle, who was in his new-used Toyota pickup and pulled up to the curb. "How will I recognize you without your old Jeep?" I asked him. He smiled and said now he's the same as every other guy in Haines who drives an old Tacoma, my husband included. The *Chilkat Valley News* garnered many awards at this spring's Alaska Press Club meeting, including "Best Small Newspaper" in the state, due to Kyle's reporting on Karl Ward.

At Mountain Market, Mary Jean, the owner, waved as she watered the flowers. Serving on the assembly is not a thankless task. Just the other day Mary Jean thanked me, and other people have, too. In this, my elders were right: send thank you notes. After I voted the way I did on the Glacier Point tour permit, George, who also organizes the Haines People for Peace group's events, sent me one and included that Howard Zinn quote. People thank me all the time for voting for the library funding and the new repairs to the pool, for assisting the Senior Village residents and agreeing with the tour operators on changes to the Borough Code that guides them, for supporting the school and for considering a police dog. I was initially opposed to the drug-sniffing dog, but after meeting with two mothers whose children ran into drug troubles and also meeting with a police officer, I'm reconsidering. If a dog could spare one family the pain of addiction or save a life, and if concerned community members have pledged to pay for its food, it may be worthwhile.

I was on my new bike again, coasting down Main to Front Street on my way over to Fort Seward. The new harbor is bigger, but there are no additional slips in the basin because there was no money left over for them. The steel breakwater and the wide rock and gravel pad for the future parking lot at the renovation project really are ugly. That was at the root of so many of my problems. Big Don's truck slowly pulled in and circled around. He must have been checking on the demolition of the former park pavilion. I wish it could have been saved, but that was another battle I lost. I think again of one of the saddest things I heard after the recall debacle was all over. I had asked Big Don why he wouldn't talk at that forum in the Chilkat Center, why he had said, "No comment," when challenged to defend his recall election. He told me it was because, "You talk too good and make me look stupid."

That's not only happening in Haines, is it? This perception that some of us are taking advantage of others by virtue of our education is a campaign strategy that apparently works, and I don't know what the remedy is. Being aware of it when I speak is a beginning. I do know that my new habit—thanks to being on the assembly—of analyzing every public comment before I make it in order to determine if my words will lead to the result I desire, is a good one no matter where or when I'm communicating. It's why I continue to write "think" and "wait" or "be quiet" at the top of my agenda even though I'm no longer nervous in the meetings. I don't want to forget this.

There are many things I wish I had done better, and some I wish I had not done at all. Sometimes I have been so certain I was right, only to realize I was wrong and had to change my mind on small judgments, such as the police dog, and larger ones, like when to say something publicly that the staff preferred be handled privately in the office. On the other hand, while I have come to appreciate the value of working behind the scenes—often it is the most effective way to influence the outcome—voters need to be in the loop, too. They need to know that their representatives are concerned about why, for example, an ordinance that no one on the assembly supports is on the agenda, and who suggested it, or hear us debate the merits of spending thousands of dollars on a new online local issue comment and survey program called OpenGov.

Tresham didn't like that idea at all, and convinced several of us that it may not be the best way to assess Haines's public opinion. Over and over again he was accused by one younger assembly member of being out of touch with the times. Of being an old fogey. Tresham always wanted us to talk about the big picture, to suspend the rules and have long open-ended conversations about our vision for our town's future. Other assembly members didn't want to meet just to talk; they felt meetings were for making decisions, not floating ideas.

Was that why Tresham chose not to run again? Well, that and maybe the recall. He missed his final assembly meeting because of his big seventy-fifth birthday party. It didn't really matter since it was only a committee meeting and the election was a few weeks away. I arrived late to his party and shook off my coat and stepped out of my boots. It was pouring rain but that big old house was warm and dry and full of friends and neighbors, and there was still plenty of food. Tresham's partner, Audrey, hadn't lit the candles on the carrot cake yet and Tresham was giving a puppet show.

He'd made the puppets with elaborately carved and painted heads. One was a mermaid and one was a witch named Esmeralda.

The best news, he said then, which is ironic now, was that since he was done with the assembly he wouldn't have "to be an adult anymore." He wore a maroon velvet and brocade jacket that fell to his knees and a necklace made of sea lion teeth. Soon he would set off on a journey, basically busking his way south, doing puppet shows out of a van. The only item on his agenda was to keep winter in the rearview mirror.

"Who will come to the puppet shows?" someone asked.

Tresham laughed and said, "Oh, probably no one, but they never do anyway, and that's fine," adding that the shows are pretty good all the same and proving it with a thoughtful short skit about peace and tolerance. Taking a puppet show on the road when you are seventy-five years old is, as Tresham would say, "very cool."

I am suddenly sorry that the story of Tresham's tenure in local government hadn't been happier. Looking back, I wish we had done more of the big-picture talk that Tresham advocated. Most of the time on the assembly is spent dealing with the business in our packets, voting, and moving on. I wish Tresham had brought those puppets and worn that jacket to at least one assembly meeting.

I wish, too, that just once our first clerk, Julie Cozzi, had followed the Pledge of Allegiance with the jazzy version of *Alaska's Flag*, our state song, like she sang on the Chilkat Center's stage, along with other local favorite tunes, in talent shows and musical reviews, which also include Tresham's puppets—that would have been wonderful. More than anything I wish I'd had the confidence to be who I was much sooner than I did when it came to governing, and that Tresham and Julie and the rest of us did not feel the pressure to conform, and wind up leaving our best qualities at home in order to appear more official, more political, more statesman-like somehow. It should be fun to be the adults who finally get to be in charge, for a little while anyway.

And it was, sometimes.

TRESHAM AND JULIE have the performance gene. I do, too, though it reveals itself in writing more than public speaking. I suspect most people who run for office have one. We would rather be on the dais than in the audience, but this trait is not one that necessarily leads to good governing. In this way, some political problems are biological. It's the nature of humans who are attracted to the political process (as well as some of those who report on it) to shout, "Look at me, look how clever I am." But it's not hopeless. The thing DNA tests don't reveal, and why even identical twins don't think and feel the same, is the nurture part— we can put ourselves in environments in which we develop new skills. People who are used to watching and observing the theater of the politics can learn to be the decision-makers, and the decision-makers can learn to listen and compromise.

From the beginning, as activist Parker J. Palmer writes, democracy has been a "nonstop experiment" in the strength and weaknesses of the system. Our form of government is just that: a guideline, the rules we collectively agree to live by. It's the people involved in it who make it work or not. Native American civil rights activist Elizabeth Peratrovich said as much when she told the Alaska Legislature in 1945 that racial segregation may be the law, but it was not right, and convinced them to change it. So much depends on people of goodwill, and they are everywhere.

When I wrote an obituary for an old gold miner, I learned he was credited with laying the first sewer line in Haines. He was tired of the stinky outhouse in the back of his favorite bar on Main Street, so one day he dug a trench and laid the pipe down to the harbor. It evolved into a proper wastewater treatment facility funded by taxpayers. When the longtime municipal sewer plant operator retired this spring, his wife told the story of how she knew she would marry him when, after their first dinner date, he gave her a tour of his workplace. He was proud of it. She loved him for that, and still does. I think about that a lot, ever since the assembly approved over a million dollars in upgrades to sewer and water systems.

There are lots of other people who change a town for the better and who, unlike Ray Menaker, Tom, Tresham, and myself, never seek or serve in elected positions. The reason we have a swimming pool in Haines is because back in the 1970s a teacher was shocked that in a waterfront, fishing community, so many people did not know how to swim. He convinced the state and local governments to supply the funds to build one. Since that time, it has literally saved the lives of boaters and commercial fishermen who were taught to swim there as children. Members of the Haines Woman's Club founded our library over eighty years ago in an abandoned shack on Main Street. Now the Haines Borough Public Library is the nicest building in town.

What we care about determines how we make our government work. We joke that Haines, because it is so small, is like a large dysfunctional family. We can disagree horribly at public hearings and write nasty letters to the editor about one another, but when someone dies, we share a pew at the funeral. At church on a recent

Sunday the priest spoke of the need for congregations and by extension communities—and I would add states and countries—to reject the current "either/or" doctrine and remember we are a "both/and" kind of place. Big Don and I are still in Haines, and so are our friends, families, and foes, so that's a victory of sorts. Maybe it's not "marvelous," but it could be otherwise. I have been accused by both critics and friends as seeing this town, and my world, through rose-colored glasses. I still do, even after everything that has happened in the last few years. Because I don't know how anyone who has ever attended a birthday potluck for an old friend, the fair, or a sunny summer wedding on the beach, with the Fishpickers—a band of fishermen playing swing tunes—and grills full of fresh salmon, and tables loaded with garden salads and home-baked breads and local beer poured from kegs, with children and dogs running all around, the best seats reserved for old people, when the Chilkat Inlet sparkles, and the mountains are impossibly huge and so close, could not believe that Haines is a preview of heaven and not be grateful that this is our life, with these people, in this place. Yes, there may be a few cracks in my lenses now, and some tape on the frame, but I choose to hold on to that vision. The view is still better from here than any other place I've been.

THERE IS ONLY a short time left until the October election when someone else can have a turn on the assembly. I'm not going to run again. There are different ways for me to do some good. Chip hasn't said "I told you so," but like his choice to be on the Haines Arts Council, a seat on the board of the watershed council sounds pretty nice right now. Along with other emotions,

I am relieved and also proud that I have participated. I think I made a positive difference in my little community. Which means anyone can—and now, more than ever, that's important. Basically, America needs volunteer EMTs and they are us.

After I got home from town earlier, I thought about all that, and about Kyle and Becky and all of us as I walked the dogs. Then I took a shower, scrambled some eggs, changed into slacks and a blouse, and rode my still-shiny new bike up the hill. Tonight's meeting began at five. Chip drove by me on his way home. He had left work early because it was a warm night and he planned to attend the Little League game with our daughters and grandchildren and treat everyone to Tex-Mex take-out.

"Will you be late?" he asked.

"I don't think so. The meeting seems pretty uncontroversial. I should be home by nine."

Which should have been my last words on this subject. I only wish.

At the very end of the meeting, under the discussion-only item on the harbor, all hell broke loose over the parking lot and sportfishing ramp construction bid process. Holy Mary, mother of God, as Teresa would say. One audience member even mentioned a recall and possible criminal charges saying that assembly members, including myself, may have illegally spoken to the contractor—Roger Schnabel, my old friend—when he called to complain about the bidding process. A staff member yelled at us, too, assuming the worst about our motives. The optics were terrible, she said. And then Brad, who had been in charge of the bids since Debra couldn't because of her conflict of interest (Roger is her brother), walked out after he said Roger questioned his integrity. When it was over, Jenna, a reporter from the *Chilkat Valley News*, stopped me on the porch and asked me what had just happened in there. I replied that it appeared to be a huge overreaction. This can't all be only about the harbor contract. However, my heart was steady and I was calm. This is all part of the process, I now know. I put my helmet on and promised I'd call tomorrow after the dust settled. Right on cue, Big Don peeled out of the parking lot, throwing grit. He was no doubt off to rally his troops.

As for me, I pedaled fast up the back of Cemetery Hill for the second time that day, but at the top I made two hard strokes, then I let go and zoomed down it in a tuck and coasted as far as I could on the flats. I pedaled lightly, just enough to stay upright and move forward, effortlessly, smoothly, quietly on that empty road alongside the inlet, below the evening sky all pink and those purple mountains. I lifted my hands off the handlebars for a few perfectly placed moments, then gripped them firmly and steered myself home.

Acknowledgments

NEARLY TWENTY YEARS ago Algonquin editor Amy Gash heard me on NPR, called me up, and asked me if I wanted to write a book. That was my lucky day. She has been my editor through four now. I am forever grateful to have had her pulling, pushing, groaning, cheering, crying, laughing, and asking good questions and patiently requesting a little (or a lot) more clarity, and always encouraging me to tell my story. Amy makes everything I write much better.

I am also grateful to Algonquin's publisher Elisabeth Scharlatt, designer Anne Winslow, managing editor Brunson Hoole, copy editor Sasha Tropp, and all the staff who made this book a reality.

Elizabeth Wales of Wales Literary Agency insisted that my term in local government was interesting enough to write about and convinced me to give it a try.

Nancy Nash and Liz Heywood, my terrific Haines-based copy editors, caught nearly every mistake and pointed them out with grace and good humor. (Any that remain are my fault.)

James Alborough provided technical and moral support.

Alekka Fullerton, Betty Holgate, Gershon Cohen, Heidi Robichaud, Kyle Clayton, Margaret Friedenauer, Mario Juarez, Melina Shields, Melissa Ganey, Ron Spatz, Ron Horn, Stephanie Scott, Teresa Hura, Tom Morphet, Tim June, Tresham Gregg, my daughter Sarah Elliott, and my sister Suzanne Vuillet-Smith offered assistance, guidance, and encouragement.

Chip is my rock and he—and our amazing evolving family of children, their spouses, and grandchildren, and all the new in-laws—makes me thankful every day for the great good fortune to be so rich in love and affection.

Beth MacCready (and our dogs) literally walked me through my term on the assembly and heard all the "rough drafts." Because she listened, there is a book. Thank you, my friend.